TEMPLES OF THE AFRICAN GODS

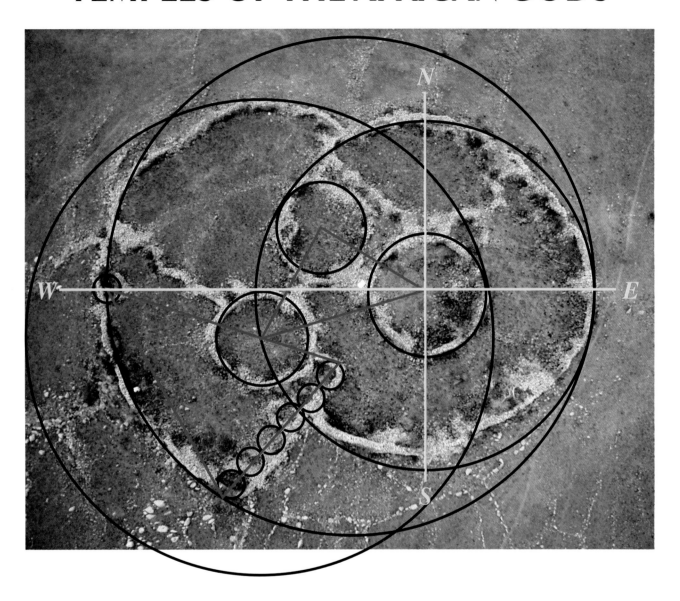

Decoding The Ancient Ruins Of Southern Africa.

Scholars have told us that the first civilisation on Earth emerged in a land called Sumer
some 6000 years ago. Recent archaeological findings suggest that the Sumerians inherited
much of their knowledge from an earlier civilisation that emerged many thousands of
years before them in southern Africa, the cradle of humankind.

By Michael Tellinger and Johan Heine

TEMPLES OF THE AFRICAN GODS

A book by Michael Tellinger
and Johan Heine

In association with the
MaKomati Foundation
Mpumalanga, South Africa

www.makomati.com

Published by Zulu Planet Publishers
PO Box 204
Waterval Boven 1195
South Africa
Contact: publisher@zuluplanet.com

© Michael Tellinger

First Edition 2009

ISBN13: 978-1-920153-08-3

Other books by Michael Tellinger:
Slave Species of god – www.slavespecies.com
Adam's Calendar – Tellinger & Heine
www.adamscalendar.com

Layout and Cover: Deep Fried Design
peter@deepfried.co.za

INTRODUCTION – ANCIENT HUMAN HISTORY

The ancient history of southern Africa is one of the great mysteries of humankind. While the world has become obsessed with places like Egypt, Mesopotamia, Mexico, and other popularised locations, very few have paid the same kind of attention to the real cradle of humankind – southern Africa. The discoveries we have been making right here since 2003 are so astonishing that they will require a dramatic paradigm shift in our perception of human history. And since history is written by the victors, it is evident that it has been dramatically skewed by its authors over many centuries. We should therefore assume that we actually know very little about the real path that brought us here. We need to set aside preconceived ideas and any rosy pictures we harbour about who we are and where we come from, because the research is delivering answers that some of us may not be ready to accept. It is imperative that we follow the clues and not hide any evidence simply because it does not fit the picture of human history, as we have painted it. This book has been compiled to simply spark the interest of those who are ready to accept a new alternative to the conventional. I am certain that there are not too many people on Earth today who are deeply happy with the way the world has turned out. A new understanding of the real history of humankind may just provide some of the answers we have been searching for and deliver a new sense of comfort for many who feel betrayed by our historians and especially by our religions.

Foreword
By Prof. Pieter Wagener

Michael and Johan are two of the bravest persons I know. Bravery can be associated with foolishness, but the bravery of this scientist and pilot stems from a conviction based on meticulous research. At the start of this millennium their findings will inaugurate a dramatic new understanding of the history of mankind over the past one hundred millennia. This understanding will affect the foundations of human understanding in all its facets, but especially in philosophy, psychology, history and religion.

Accordingly, their bravery will be put to severe test. Innovators are rarely appreciated and gratitude takes a long time in coming. One may therefore wonder why they should go to all the trouble? But that is the stuff a true scientist is made of.

When the reader looks at the photographs in this book his first reaction would be: Why has no one before taken a serious look at these thousands of structures and petroglyphs? Because we become complacent when other people tell us that there is nothing significant about them. Michael and Johan are about to demolish that complacency and make every reader, believer or not, uncomfortable about the origins of our civilisation. Even worse, the reader could deduce that some of our ancestors have been much smarter than we are today.

Ex Africa semper aliquid novi (Out of Africa always something new).

Pieter Wagener
BA MSc MA MSc LLM PhD LLD

Visionaries

Sanusi Credo Mutwa – an unsung hero who has been a guiding light of wisdom for millions of people on this confused planet

Credo's reminder of Africa's great hidden legacy

Scholars have told us that the first civilisation on Earth emerged in a land called Sumer, between the rivers Tigris and Euphrates, some 6000 years ago. Recent archaeological discoveries suggest that the Sumerians and even the Egyptians inherited much of their knowledge from an earlier civilisation that emerged many thousands of years before in southern Africa, the cradle of humankind.

Sanusi Credo Mutwa is probably South Africa's most treasured visionary, Shaman and Sangoma. For many years Credo has been talking about the ancient civilisations that existed here in South Africa and caused many so-called educated scholars to scoff at his statements. When Johan Heine discovered the ancient stone calendar (Adam's Calendar) at Kaapschehoop, South Africa in 2003, he could never have imagined that this would be the spark that started the sudden emergence of archaeological proof to vindicate the statements of Baba Credo.

Our proof comes in the form of large stone monolith statues, petroglyphs and symbols, discovered in Mpumalanga and other parts of South Africa, which were previously believed to be of Sumerian and Egyptian origins. Our conclusions are not only based on the many convincing artefacts we have accumulated and the staggering ages ascribed to them, but also on the transcripts of the Sumerian tablets themselves. These tablets are the oldest written record of human history and the constant reference to southern Africa in these tablets, leaves little doubt that there was a lot of activity here, long before Sumer or Egypt were established. It is now very clear that the first civilisation emerged many thousand of years ago in a land the Sumerians called the ABZU – the land of the FIRST people in southern Africa – where the gold came from.

Above: A Sumerian cross – just one of thousands of ancient petroglyphs at Driekopseiland, not far from Kimberley, South Africa. Carved into a flat black glaciated slab of Andesite, one of the hardest rocks known. This cross is just one example of the same symbols that are found all over the world. In ancient African tradition this symbol represents Mabona – the Lord of Light.

Hidden History

Above: An Egyptian Ankh carved into a glacier slab at Dreikopseiland, South Africa. This petroglyph is worth a thousand words since the Ankh is inside a radiating circle; suggesting that the Lord of Light has the key to eternal life. It also suggests that the secret lies in the frequency of light or is linked to some kind of vibrational energy that combines sound and light. This knowledge would be consistent with the circular ruins of southern Africa that were used to generate energy by using sound and possibly also light. This understanding of the flow of energy in sound and light was rediscovered by Keely, Tesla and Rife in the late 20th century.

Right: The Ankh is one the most recognised symbols of ancient Egypt. It represents the key to eternal life and knowledge.

The quest for our human origins has led scholars and explorers down some fascinating paths. The past two centuries have seen giant leaps in scientific technology that has allowed researchers to present some remarkable conclusions. It must be hastily added that most of what we have been presented with so far about our human origins, are only theories and hypotheses based on the latest information gathered by the messengers. It is a common mistake by people outside the areas of research to believe some of these scientific theories to be the absolute final word on the subject. This process of misinformation often starts because it is presented by the media who get the facts all messed up, and before we know it, everybody believes it.

History has taught us that humans, and especially the appointed leaders of the establishment, do not take kindly to change and new information. All we have to do is look at some of the great discoveries of the past few centuries to realise how stubborn and arrogant we can be about our personal deep seeded belief systems. Many discoveries have been met with fierce resistance, especially by religious leaders and so-called scholars who in reality should be promoting the concept of progress. Countless books have been written about the covering up of new discoveries because they did not fit the pretty picture held by authorities of the time. And if you think that this is how it happened in the past, and today we are all well informed by the beloved media, you are not only incredibly naïve, but grossly mistaken.

Think of Galileo who was forced to retract his scientific findings about our solar system. He was placed under house arrest and tortured until he apologised and retracted his statements. It took about another 100 years for his theories to be accepted. Just cast your mind back to the first flight of the Wright brothers in 1903, which probably happened much earlier but could not be unleashed on the people of the time because the expert scientists of the time insisted that "man could not fly a heavier-than-air machine". The fantastic discoveries of Nikola Tesla and his free energy; Royal Raymond Rife who found "the cure for all disease" and in 1931 demonstrated how to cure cancer at will in a laboratory. Around 1888 John Keely demonstrated his anti-gravity device; sound vibration machines that could drill stone of any density with absolute perfection, and even vibrational fields that could completely crush giant granite megaliths to the finest powder in just a few seconds. These discoveries were covered up so well that they were completely removed from the broader knowledge pool and remain so today.

Tesla, Rife and Keely should have changed history dramatically and yet they mysteriously faded into mediocrity. During the course of exploration we are often presented with evidence and information outside our scope of comprehension that goes against everything we have been taught. But this is after all what true science and discovery is all about. It has no limits and it is forever changing. The only constant in science is 'change'. Our immediate knee-jerk response is to often reject new information because we have 'never heard about it before'. I trust you will agree that this is not a scientific argument, and never will be.

Most of us know Albert Einstein as the genius who answered many of our questions about space-time and the speed of light. But Einstein himself pushed the boundaries of possibility like all true scientists. Very few of us are aware of the bulk of his work and one of his favourite subjects which was called "spooky action at a distance". It basically shows how two particles separated by extreme distance and no connection between them of any nature, still remain connected by some invisible force. When one of the particles is stimulated and responds in a specific way, the other particle also displays the same immediate response, across a vast distance, faster than the speed of light. This part of his research, which included the

Nikola Tesla

Royal Raymond Rife

John Keely – Just like Tesla and Rife, he realised that sound is a prime creative source, and can be used for most applications imaginable when truly understood.

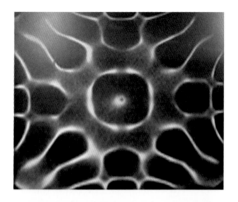

Left: Experiments at Harvard University show how sound energy creates patterns in sand. Low frequencies seem to create more basic circular patterns, while higher frequencies make more complex patterns. Interfering frequencies cause strange complex patterns. The rule is quite simple – every frequency of energy manifests in a very unique pattern.

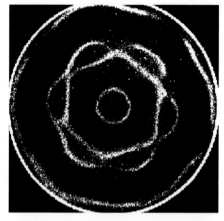

Left: This is the pattern created by the vibrational energy of the vowel "A". Notice the circle in the middle and that the outer circle is not perfectly round, but has a wave-like shape around the perimeter.

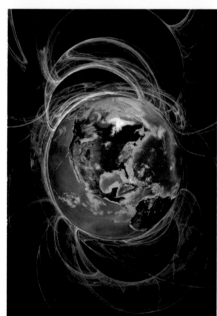

Above: Computer generated energy fields emanating from Earth all over its surface. This is what Tesla most likely tapped into to convert into his free energy.

Tesla did thousands of experiments as part of his research. He showed that the Earth is "alive" with currents of energy that surface in various frequencies everywhere. He realised that this energy can be used to power any apparatus imaginable, and for any application imaginable. This energy did not need wires to be conducted, it was carried in the particles and molecules of air in a way that was not understood before. The Earth acted like a capacitor for this energy – an inexhaustible storage device that could provide any amount of energy needed anywhere. It is obvious that this kind of easy access to free energy was not well received by the controlling electricity giants. It was not long before they destroyed everything Tesla had invented and the FBI confiscated his patents because of his financial debts.

Philadelphia experiment in July 1943 has been very successfully ridiculed and covered up to a large extent.

Max Planck, the father of quantum physics is another Nobel Prize winner who had a very advanced view of the universe, but once again his 'other' work is underplayed and ridiculed to a large extent. Planck was fascinated by the concept of the "Matrix", which was an expression that emerged from the world of hardcore physics, and not some Hollywood script writer. He believed that the universe is connected by an invisible matrix grid of energy, to which we are all connected through an invisible grid of consciousness. We therefore all share a collective memory and knowledge which is held in this matrix – not in our brains. In 1933 Paul Dirac won the Nobel Prize for physics, when he showed that all matter in the universe originates from a source of gamma-ray light or energy. This matter emerges from the subatomic singularity state of non-dual particles that eventually make up the whole universe and all the stuff in it. Gamma-ray light crosses the whole universe in an instant, which could explain "spooky action at a distance". Greg Braden is an American scientist and author who has done much research on this subject and published several highly informative books. What I find fascinating about this discovery,

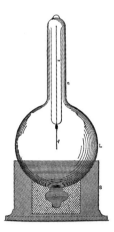

Above: Tesla's wireless light bulb. His light bulb was just one example of tapping into the Earth as energy device. It had no wires and simply drew the energy from the hand of the person who held it. Some of the light bulbs did not even need a touch from a person, but simply lit up when a person was within close proximity.

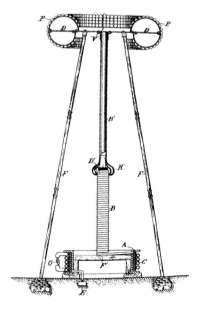

Above: One of the hundreds of patents of Nikola Tesla (1914) – the man that should have changed the world. A device for transmitting electric energy – without wires. Note that Tesla called it radiant, non-polar ENERGY, and not electricity. Therein lies a major clue for those who are trying to emulate his work.

Left: The Tesla Tower in Long Island New York. It was from this tower that Tesla beamed the free energy that could power people's homes and cars, without any wires. When his sponsor, J.P. Morgan, realised that this energy could not be measured or easily controlled, he stopped his funding of any future projects, demolished the tower and the FBI confiscated all documentation. Morgan ended up owning the giant hydro-electric power plants in North America. To this day, no-one has been able to emulate Tesla's free energy and his methods remain a great mystery to all scientists. Tesla reportedly removed the engine from a convertible, replaced it with a black box of some sort, placed an aerial sticking out the back seat of the car, and drove the car around Long Island for about six weeks without any petrol – just powered by the energy beamed from the Tesla Tower. (Source of picture – unknown)

is that it fits the long-held belief that the speed of light is actually not a barrier to travel, but the stuff that makes up light is the actual mechanism for travelling beyond the speed of light.

So as we explore the ancient stone ruins of South Africa and keep bumping into mysterious, inexplicable 'stuff' and ponder its origins, we need to keep all of this in mind. We are uncovering vanished civilisations, of which we have no knowledge at all. We are knocking on the door of our human origins, and what we find, is not always what we had expected to find. There are many questions and only

a few hypothetical answers based on our current pool of accumulated knowledge. I have been studying human origins for over two decades and there is only one conclusion that I have been able to reach in all this time. Things are not as they seem and as soon as you begin to dig into the unknown past, you very quickly realise that hidden below the sands of time is a completely different history of humankind. A past that has somehow been hidden from view over thousands of years. The deeper we dig and the more we ask, the more convinced we become that what we have been told is not necessarily the absolute truth.

Human Origins & Mythology

While the true origins of humankind are still very murky and entangled in a never-ending tussle between evolutionists and creationists, there are fascinating clues left behind by ancient civilisations that point us in a very specific direction. All of this activity in the distant past cannot be separated from religion. Many ancient religious scripts that have survived from various corners of the world give us remarkable clarity on a multitude of issues. One such issue is the presence of a group of ever-present and omni-present gods and deities with advanced powers that seemed to have ruled the world for thousands of years. These gods were led by a mysterious pantheon of 12 gods that seems to be present in every ancient civilisation, scattered across all the continents, separated by thousands of miles. Those who hold the Bible dear should not be surprised to find that these same deities and gods are referred to in the Bible on many occasions.

In the original Bible, before it was translated and streamlined, the original word for God was Elohim – which is a plural word meaning Gods. This was always the case and the biblical God has always been a plural – Gods. Suddenly the many references by God to himself in the plural, like "let us create man in our image" and "let us go down and confuse their language" become less confusing.

And when we realise that most of the stories from Genesis and Exodus are translations from their original source written in the Sumerian tablets, it all starts to make a lot more sense. The same gods that the Sumerian tablets refer to, are the same plural Gods that are mentioned in the Bible. All the greatest biblical stories have their origins in the Sumerian tablets.

While the story is often reduced to one line in the Bible, the original Sumerian texts are written in much greater detail: The seven tablets of creation of heaven and Earth; creation of Adamu – the biblical Adam; creation of Eve from Adamu's rib; the garden of Edin; the serpent and the tree of knowledge and life; the flood; Noah (Ziusudra) and the ark; destruction of Sodom and Gomorra; the tower of Babel and its destruction by the gods, and many more. These tales are all well documented by the Sumerians and some of these tablets pre-date the Bible by as much as 3,000 years.

It is also important to note that in Sumerian, Egyptian, Greek, and all other cultures, the gods are never referred to as imaginary – but as very, very real. They interacted with the people, they informed the people and they punished the people. The first so-called holy trinity arose in Sumeria. It was Anu, the father and his two sons Enlil and Enki, who ruled the roost on planet Earth. We know that Enlil was given the northern half of the planet to look after and Enki who was also known as the creator god or serpent, was in charge of the southern part of the planet. They were supported by an extended family of a total of 12 central deities, each with special tasks and responsibilities. The Sumerian tablets refer to them

Left: The Caduceus – well-known as the symbol of the medical profession. Its origin goes back thousands of years to the symbol of the Sumerian deity Enki, who was known as the winged serpent or flying serpent, the creator of the human race and the god of medicine and healing. The winged serpent is worshipped by virtually every ancient civilisation as their creator god, and serpent worship is associated with the creation of humans.

as the powerful Anunnaki and their sons the Nephilim, while the Bible calls them Anakim (giants), the descendants of the Nephilim – who are also referred to as the sons of the gods in Genesis.

Genesis 6:4
The Nephilim were on the earth in those days—and also afterward—when the sons of God (the gods) went to the daughters of men and had children by them. They were the heroes of old, men of renown.

This pantheon of ancient powerful gods or beings was also very active and very present right here in South Africa under their leader Enki. The evidence is everywhere, especially in the many references of the Sumerian tablets.

This leads us directly into one of the most misunderstood and misused expressions of our time. This seemingly innocuous word has caused much confusion in our modern times and caused us to completely misunderstand all of human history. The word is 'mythology'. The original meaning in Greek had nothing to do with 'imaginary'. In fact it seems to be quite the opposite. The original meaning of 'mythos' was: *words, written words; spoken words; legend and*

Right: Zeus fights his brother Hades for control of Earth. Hades is depicted as the winged serpent, who is banished to the underworld. This is also the story of the Sumerian deity brothers Enlil and Enki. Enlil took control of the upper world while Enki, the winged serpent, took control of the underworld. This was the land below the equator – where the gold came from. NOT hell, as is often misinterpreted. Sumerians called this place ABZU.

tales of historic accounts sworn to be true by kings and priests.

Can you see the problem here? What was taken to be part of the daily life of ancient people, has been reduced to imaginary fairy tales by modern historians. According to my research, it was around 1270 AD that the meaning of the word 'mythological' was first misused and has subsequently created immense damage in all future history books.

Is it possible that all ancient civilisations never had a real history, real experiences, and real religion? Is it possible that they just imagined things because they could not understand the

big bad world around them? This is exactly what some historians would like us to believe. Once we realise that mythology actually means 'history' the whole picture changes quite dramatically. We suddenly realise that in the distant past there was a group of powerful beings (gods) that controlled events all over the planet, including southern Africa. This is instantly recognisable in the symbols and statues carved in rock, in South Africa, that pre-date the Egyptian and Sumerian equivalent. It is important that the presence of these ancient so-called gods, should not be confused with the true creator of the universe and all things in it – the GOD with a big G.

Cornerstones Of Our Beliefs

There are thousands of religions and belief systems on Earth. Many are off-shoots from ancient religions and belief systems. Christianity alone has over 20,000 sects that all seem to have a slightly different take on the whole thing. I have identified three common denominators that are shared by all people and every civilisation on Earth as far back as we can push the human envelope of history. They are gold, slavery and the feathered serpent or winged/flying serpent. These are truly fascinating when analysed in detail and cannot be separated from human history.

GOLD: No matter how far back in time we search, gold has always somehow played a part in human activity. It was however not only humankind, but also their gods, that have been obsessed with gold. Even in the book of Genesis, God expresses his own obsession for this shiny metal. It makes no sense at all why ancient *Homo sapiens* and their creator would have been so consumed by gold before the appearance of currency or trade. For those who are keen to explore this further, I cover this subject and the real reasons for mankind's quest for gold in great detail in my book *Slave Species of god.*

SLAVERY: Has been practised by mankind as far back as we can go. Even God's chosen people, according to the Bible, were enslaved by others. It is interesting to note that the ancient gods, which include the Gods of the Bible and Koran, not only condoned the practice of slavery, but gave the slave masters precise instructions on how to treat their slaves, how to punish their slaves, and under which circumstances they may kill their slaves. Why and how early humans stumbled upon the concept of slavery defies any logic, but rather suggests that humankind was taught this unsavoury activity by someone with a prior knowledge of it.

THE WINGED SERPENT: The winged or feathered serpent is regarded as the creator god in almost every ancient civilisation. It was this so-called mythical creature that arrived out of the sky, created the people, gave them all their knowledge for survival, and punished them if they misbehaved. From the Sumerians to the Chinese, the North Americans, Mesoamericans and South Americans, South Africa to Egypt, serpent worship has always been a part of ancient civilisations.

Most of these tribes still use feathers in their traditional clothing and ritual dances, not realising that this is actually a reference to the feathered serpent and their creator god from thousands of years ago. African culture is no different. Ancient Zulu tradition tells us of the 'Abelungu' – great white sky gods, or 'heaven dwellers' who once lived on Earth. They came from the blue sky on giant wings and they could go back to heaven in a flash of light. They created the Zulu people and gave them life and knowledge, which included the working of gold.

It is truly curious that the symbol used by modern medicine today is the same ancient symbol used by the earliest Sumerian civilisation to represent their creator ENKI – who was also referred to as a medical master with a knowledge of life and death, and the caretaker of the first gold mines. So, by the time the greedy explorers from Europe arrived here, the gold mining civilisation was already well developed and had been flourishing for thousands of years. But so was the dark practice of slavery. For at least five centuries before, Africa was well entrenched in this unsavoury business, of selling humans as property. According to experts, the ports of Mozambique had exported large numbers of African slaves to the rest of the world. It seems that Africa has always been the inexhaustible source of slaves. How did this come about and why?

One of the many stone walls that still stands close to three metres high. A section of a large ruin with a diameter of 150 metres. A carved stone that resembles a human head stands close by, as if it was part of some kind of ritual. Many strange and inexplicable carved shapes of stone are found scattered among the ruins, accompanied by hundreds of strange stone tools that were previously not recognised as stone tools.

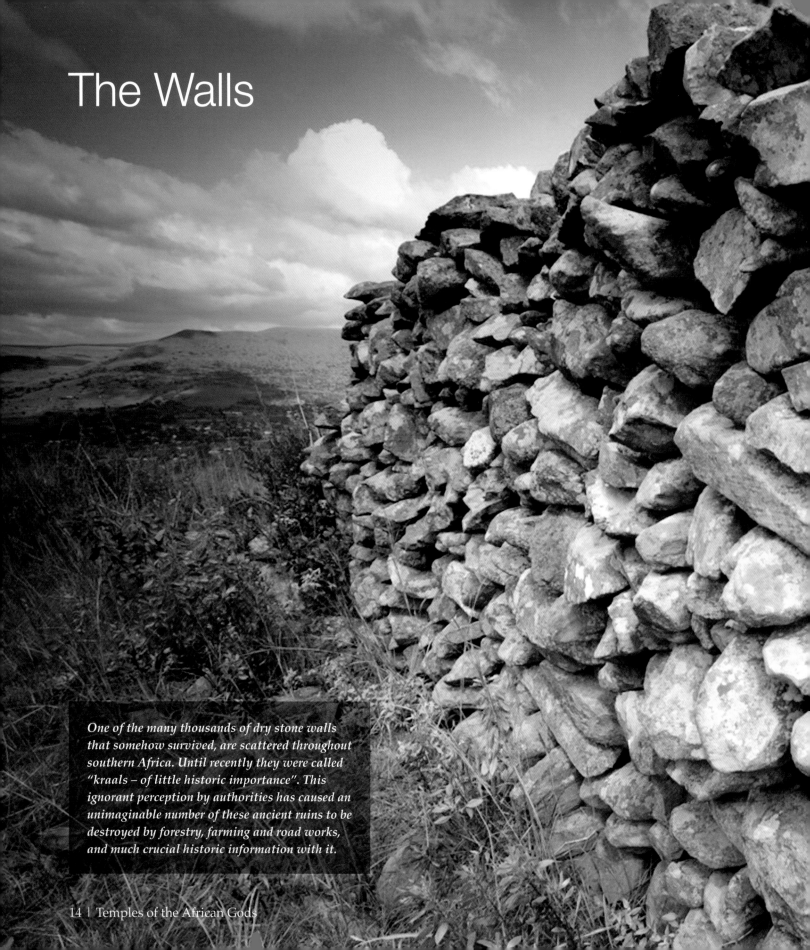

The Walls

One of the many thousands of dry stone walls that somehow survived, are scattered throughout southern Africa. Until recently they were called "kraals – of little historic importance". This ignorant perception by authorities has caused an unimaginable number of these ancient ruins to be destroyed by forestry, farming and road works, and much crucial historic information with it.

We call this ruin the Stone Window, high on a mountain, part of a large ruin. Since it faces east, the window is most likely an alignment for one of the solstices or equinox. It may also align with a specific star on the horizon – more research is necessary.

The fascination with the ancient stone ruins in southern Africa goes back many centuries. Dozens of explorers, some of whom were simply greedy treasure hunters, have derived fame with their accounts of braving the savages of Africa to conquer the dark continent. In some social circles, these stone ruins of the south have mesmerised explorers as much as the pyramids of Egypt. But because Egypt is so often referred to as a great lost civilisation, we often forget that Egypt is actually also in Africa. It is remarkable, that in essence, we are looking at two great civilisations at the opposite ends of the continent.

Make no mistake, the discovery of this vanished civilisation at the southern tip of Africa holds even more mystery than its northern cousin. It has more undeciphered mythology; countless stone ruins of unknown origin; great kings and wise men of the past; Shamans and Sangomas of the present who have upheld ancient tradition and preserved ancient knowledge; and most importantly, the same pantheon of gods who ruled all over the planet. The common links that we have identified leave no doubt that southern Africa did not escape the attention of the ancient gods. It is however very clear that the relationship those gods had with the ABZU (southern Africa) was quite different from their activities in other parts of the planet. It is very sad that we will never

know the full extent of what was originally found at the most impressive ruins in southern Africa when they were first discovered by the colonialists from the north. The destruction and plundering that took place at these ruins will never be fully realised. It is certain that all valuable items were carted off by those who first found them and not much consideration was given to their significance. Monoliths were removed and pushed aside without measuring their alignments with stars or their orientation to the cardinal points of Earth. This was certainly the case at Mapungupwe, the most famous of the South African sites, where the one-horned golden rhino was discovered. Luckily the golden rhino and other gold artefacts did survive. What was finally reported from these early sites is far from the truth and we must not allow that information to skew our judgement.

During 2008 a very important event took place. The Head of the University of Pretoria and a bunch of their archaeologists were forced to apologise

Right: Sections of walls in different ruins – some walls have thick lichen growing on them while others have moss, or both. There are a few different building styles indicating that they were built during different periods and altered by later arrivals. The oldest ones always display the same basic circular design – with no entrances.

to the indigenous people of Limpopo, for the desecration of Mapungupwe and various other sacred ancient sites. They promised to return most of the artefacts that were removed from the sites over the past 60+ years, but were unable to account for many artefacts that had mysteriously vanished, such as a very large diamond which was among the items removed by archaeologists.

One of the first documented entries that describe large stone ruins in the fabled kingdom of Monomotapa, which would be central to northern Zimbabwe today, was made around 1512 AD by a Portuguese convict-turned-explorer called Antonio Fernandes. Even at this point in time the stone structures were in ruin, completely overgrown and deserted. Fernandes was just one of many convicted criminals called "degradados" who were given the option to go to Africa to explore the 'dangerous dark continent' for their European monarchs and report back on their findings… if they survived. It seems that the European kings and clergy of the time all had the same plan of action. They would send in the great unwashed to discover hidden treasures, only to send in the troops soon after to rape the land of all its wealth and enslave the natives. The early explorers caused death and destruction among the natives in all corners of the so-called new worlds, the Americas, Africa and India. This was all done in the name of God and greed, and always with the blessing of the pope.

In 1552, his successor Joao de Barros, wrote about large mysterious stone ruins. He also described a lintel above the entrance with inscriptions that

Opposite Page: From the grass among the ruins we have no idea that this is part of a large complex on top of a mountain linked by roads and other peculiar structures. Note, that in all the ruins, without exception, the original stones are not part of the natural stone in the area but are brought in from some distance away. Geologists agree that most of the stones seem to have their origin in river beds because of their rounded smooth shapes.

Top: Another stunning example of a wall that still stands 3 metres high. What cannot be seen from the ground is the road that runs into the structure. These stones come from a river bed about 2km down the mountain.

Right: Close up of a small section of a wall indicating the large size of some of the stones. This large one weighs about 200 – 300 kg. Not the kind of stone you would want to carry up the mountain from the nearest river. So how and why did they go to so much trouble to do just that?

Photo: Gustav Janse van Rensburg – Rock & Rope

Top: Michael Tellinger points out the height of the wall. This is one of the well-preserved ruins which was measured and found to be aligned with many celestial aspects by Johan Heine.

Left: A good example of reconstruction by latter inhabitants who adapted the stone structure for their own needs – with doors and square shapes which indicate more recent usage. The rule is quite simple – when you see square structures, it means it was used by westerners or European arrivals since the 15th century AD.

Right: A spectacular effect of walls upon walls. This spectacular ruin near Waterval Boven was built from an estimated 500,000 stones, all brought up from the river in the valley. Current explanations are that this was built by a small family or two consisting of no more than 14 people. Our calculation concludes that it would be impossible for such a small group of people to complete this structure in one lifetime.

Bottom right: One of the many unexplained stones that are built into the walls. They were probably part of some ritual or alignment as yet not understood.

could not be deciphered, even by the learned Moors who knew many languages. What is really curious about this event is that these Moorish wise men could not even identify the script, which was carved into the lintel. Sadly, this precious lintel has long since mysteriously disappeared. It is important to remember that the local tribes did not have a written language at this time in history, and yet there were inscriptions above an entrance to their ruins. From the written entries it is clear that de Barros and the Moors knew with certainty that these ruins

were there for the purpose of extracting gold. When de Barros asked the local tribes of the area about the original builders, he was told that it must have been built by the devil, because "… it does not seem possible that they should be the work of man." (Summers 1971)

Modern historians and academics have rushed to place a date on the building of these stone structures and automatically assume that they must have been built by the people living in the area, or at worse, their immediate

Top left: Michael Tellinger crouches below a large rock that is part of a stone wall completely covered by soil. The entire complex is overgrown by trees and undergrowth so that it cannot be seen from the ground by hikers nor from a helicopter when hunting for ruins as we often do. To truly understand the huge expanse of the ruins in southern Africa, we had to walk many mountains and crawl into many overgrown bush areas to discover the hidden ruins that cover the landscape, but remain invisible.

Centre top: The vast expanse of a ruined city near Rustenburg, South Africa. This is one of the three lost cities that we identified, covering about 10,000 km square – larger than modern Johannesburg or Los Angeles. All the stones were brought from elsewhere, near the river bed, since they do not form part of the natural bedrock.

Bottom Left: One of many mysterious circular passages surrounding a stone circle, that has no entrance nor exit – it simply ends in walls in all directions.

Top Right: Examples of large stones in massive walls that are over 1,5m wide, part of the lost city of Rustenburg. Some of these stones weigh well over 150kg. A construction of this size is not a simple task, considering that all the stones had to be brought from some distance away – sometimes more than 3km away.

Left: Outer wall of another ruin with several internal structures.

Top: A picture from 1939 shows a small hut-like structure completely constructed from stone slabs. The bottom picture shows the structure today with collapsed roof. There is as yet no feasible explanation for the purpose of such a structure – all the obvious ones seem to apply our modern values that just don't fit any of our findings associated with these ancient civilisations. There are many such ruins, indicating very small circular stone enclosures that defy any modern logic.

Left: This is a great example of the high levels of destruction that some ruins exhibit. The large stones can be seen close to camera. For forces of nature to cause such high levels of decay would take a very long time and possibly some serious environmental disasters like a great flood. There is no reason or evidence to suggest that these structures were destroyed by other tribes.

A view of a ruined wall in the foreground, and more ruined circles on the adjacent hill. The hills and mountains are covered with stone ruins. To the untrained eye they are mostly invisible but examples like these are a good indicator of what this part of the world looked like many thousands of years ago. Great Zimbabwe on the right is no exception – walls in the foreground and ruined Acropolis on the hill in the distance. This mysterious ruin is part of the three lost cities we have discovered in southern Africa and its structure is identical to the millions of other ruins. The grand entrance of Great Zimbabwe below remains an awesome sight.

Photo: Bill Maliepaard

Photo: Bill Maliepaard

ancestors. I would assume that if 'their' ancestors could write, 'they' would be able to write too, and not lose such a precious ability. This was not the case however. So who were these advanced mysterious people who could write and build impressive stone structures like Great Zimbabwe? Where did they disappear to, and when?

The migration of the Bantu people from the north, into this region of southern Africa, especially Zimbabwe, and later into South Africa, remains a hotly debated subject. Many speculations and theories are thrown around. While some claim that this event can be traced to around the year zero, others argue it cannot be traced further back than about 1200 AD. For many years it has been suggested that the arrival of the Bantu, and later the Europeans, caused the demise of the Bushman or Khoisan, who were driven from their ancestral lands. These theories keep changing and have changed again in the past few years. It is now speculated that the Khoi arrived in South Africa from eastern Africa around 2,000 years ago. It is therefore argued that many or most of the rock engravings associated with this group cannot be older than 2,000 years.

This is just another silly example of the reverse application of logic. In science, we cannot force the evidence to fit our theories and yet this is what I keep stumbling upon in my research as an independent scientist. Our theories should be formulated from the evidence we find. Any seasoned archaeologist should be

Section of a large ruin overlooking adjacent hills. As far as you can see, the hills were once covered with structures like these.

able to see very quickly from the erosion that the so-called Khoisan petroglyphs are many thousands of years old by simply observing the cracks that have formed through some of them.

These theories about the arrival of the Bantu and Khoi people from the north suggest that southern Africa was an empty land until they arrived here. Yet millions of stone tools have been discovered and many more lie beneath the sand. How many Homo erectus or Homo habilis lived here in ancient times to have needed all these millions of tools? Countless ruined stone dwellings lie scattered throughout the lands without any attention from academics. It is time for our historians to wake up and face reality – deal with the evidence and not just conveniently shove it under the carpet.

Current history books and government papers categorically state that South Africa was very sparsely populated by small groups of migrating people from the north until the early 1700s. There is still much debate about the events surrounding the migration of the early settlers into southern Africa and the arrival of Bantu people, the Khoi and the San are still very speculative. Some scholars continue to insist that the stone structures of Zimbabwe and South Africa could not have been built before the settlement of the Bantu people in this part of Africa. This is another clear case of forcing the data to fit the existing theory, while the evidence of an earlier, vanished African civilisation surrounds us everywhere.

To emphasize the levels of confusion, I insert an extract from the South African Government Info website. According to this paper, the Khoi and the San have been present in southern Africa for an uncertain period.

"The early inhabitants
The discovery of the skull of a Taung child in 1924; discoveries of hominid fossils at Sterkfontein caves, a world heritage site; and the ground-breaking work done at Blombos Cave in the southern Cape, have all put South Africa at the forefront of palaeontological research into the origins of humanity. Modern humans have lived in the region for over 100,000 years.

The small, mobile bands of Stone-Age hunter-gatherers, who created a wealth of rock art, were the ancestors of the Khoikhoi and San of historical times. The Khoikhoi and San (the "Hottentots" and "Bushmen" of early European terminology), although collectively known as the Khoisan, are often thought of as distinct peoples.

The former were those who, some 2,000 years ago, adopted a pastoralist lifestyle herding sheep and later, cattle. Whereas the hunter-gatherers adapted to local environments and were scattered across the subcontinent, the herders sought out the pasturelands between modern-day Namibia and the Eastern Cape, which, generally, are near the coast. At around the same time, Bantu-speaking agropastoralists began arriving in southern Africa, bringing with them an iron-age culture and domesticated crops. After establishing themselves in the well-watered eastern coastal region of southern Africa, these farmers spread out across the interior plateau, or "highveld", where they adopted a more extensive cattle-farming culture."

The mystery of the stone ruins lingers. The inexplicable elements are the large numbers of ruins and settlements; the sheer size of the area they cover; the hundreds of kilometres of ancient roads; thousands of large stone monoliths and statues aligned to many celestial and geographic elements; thousands of kilometres of agricultural terraces; and the size of the population required to have built all these structures.

From the accounts of Joao de Barros it is much more feasible that the mysterious inscription at Great Zimbabwe was not the work of the new African settlers from the north, who most likely just occupied the structure, but an earlier southern African civilisation, who were well evolved in the art of building with stone, and more importantly, a people who had the knowledge of writing.

Top: Part of a mud hut wall remains inside a large stone circle. Clear indication how later arrivals adapted the ruins for their own needs. Many examples like this have been found. This has caused some scholars to believe that the circular stone structures were built by the same people who then constructed the mud huts inside. No evidence to support such theories has been produced. What these discoveries show is proof of habitation of recent occupants – not proof of constructions of the original stone structure.

Centre: Part of a Stone Age structure with a flat stone altar against one of the walls. Several tools from the Middle Stone Age have been found here.

Bottom: Small section of a very different style of wall building, using mud as mortar between the stones. This lies about 30m from the ruin above, showing once again how civilisations build on top of each other, re-using the materials from the previous inhabitants.

Obsession With The Stars

A 3D reconstruction of Adam's Calendar, showing the Horus statue and three Orion stones – aligned perfectly to the rise of Orion's belt, on the vernal equinox, when it was flat on the horizon. Current calculations indicate that this would have occurred at least 160,000 years ago. More measurements and calculations are necessary.

Virtually all ancient civilisations were obsessed with the stars. They observed them, they worshipped them, they tracked their movement, they depicted them in art and rock engravings, and carved images of celestial beings from stone.

Their knowledge of the cosmos was astounding. The Maya civilisation from Mesoamerica is possibly the best example of this with their variety of precise calendars, which can measure time and cosmic events for millions of years into the past

and the future. They knew about the 26,000-year precessional wobble of planet Earth and their long count calendar is based on this time period. They also knew that the constellations of Scorpio and Sagittarius point to the centre of our galaxy, the Milky

Way. It was only in the latter part of the 20th century when scientists began to realise that these ancient people had a much more advanced knowledge of the cosmos than we have, and more scientists are joining this group of believers on a daily basis.

The most frequent star systems linked with life on Earth are Sirius, the Pleiades and Orion's Belt. While Orion played a major part in the alignments and construction of the Giza pyramids, the Mayan pyramids, the Chinese pyramids and even Great Zimbabwe, it is Sirius that has caused many surprises. It is also the key star in the construction of the Great Pyramid, while the Egyptian Sothic calendar is based on the same star. The second of the two southern shafts of the Great Pyramid points to Orion. It is believed that these shafts represent the ascension of the Pharaoh's soul to the source of life, which was believed to be Orion and Sirius. This is just a tiny taste of the vast ancient knowledge of the cosmos.

And if you think that this advanced knowledge of the cosmos was not present among the ancient tribes of southern Africa, you are grossly mistaken. This obsession is deeply entrenched in ancient southern African tradition. According to

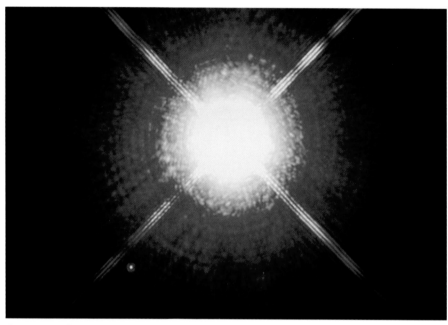

Sirius A with its tiny binary partner Sirius B to the bottom left.

Mutwa there are various 'star tribes' in Africa that carry great star knowledge and the Ndebele people are the ones who carry the ancient knowledge of the *Mbube* star of Orion – the Far-walking Constellation or *Umhabi*. Johan Heine's meticulous exploratory work at *Adam's Calendar* has shown that these ancient civilisations in the south were in touch with the stars long before anyone else. While our first calculations showed Adam's Calendar has been aligned with the rise of Orion's Belt on the spring equinox some 75,000 years ago, the latest calculations point to a date well over 160,000 years. Much more measuring needs to be done and I am certain that

we will find a clear link to Sirius very soon, for the simple reason that Credo suggests that life on Earth originated from the Sirius planetary system. And so far, he has not been wrong about much.

The Dogon people of Mali is another African 'star tribe' of ancient cultures who shows an uncanny knowledge of cosmic affairs. The Dogon belief is that life on Earth came from Sirius and this has been part of their custom for thousands of years. They have always known that the brightest star in the sky, Sirius, has a twin, Sirius-B. They also knew that our Sun was actually part of the Sirius binary system, as a third star. This has also only very recently become

Eastern view of a 3D reconstruction of Adam's Calendar. The oldest version of the Egyptian Horus hawk stands in line with the Spring Equinox sunrise. To the right are the 3 aligned stones of Orion. Further up in the top right corner you can see the faint outline of the 2 pyramids also aligned with Orion's rise. The pyramids are directly aligned with Great Zimbabwe and the Great Pyramid of Giza in Egypt, along 31 degrees east longitude.

known to a small enlightened group of astrophysicists. The Dogon priests claimed that Sirius had a companion star, which was invisible to the human eye. They also said that the star moved in a 50-year elliptical orbit around Sirius. They said that it rotated on its axis, it was white, small and that it was the 'heaviest star'.

This information was only recently discovered by modern astronomers who in 1844 began to suspect that Sirius-A, had a companion star. This was determined when they realised that the path of the star was irregular and wobbly. In 1862 Alvan Clark discovered the second star confirming that Sirius was indeed a binary star system of two stars. In the 1920s it was determined that Sirius-B, the companion of Sirius, was a white dwarf star, smaller than planet Earth. White dwarfs are

small, dense stars that burn dimly with an extremely high gravity. It is this gravity pull that causes the wobbly, wavy movement of Sirius-A. The Dogon name for Sirius-B is **Po Tolo**, which can be translated as 'smallest seed – Po; and 'Tolo – star'. The seed refers to creation and the seeding of Earth from Sirius.

For thousands of years the Dogon have attributed three

principal properties to Sirius-B: small, heavy, white. This is not something we can conveniently shove under the carpet as some scholars often prefer to do because they do not want to deal with the mystery. We have to be sober about this and attempt to get to the true origins of this knowledge pool. How could this seemingly primitive tribe from Africa have possibly known this?

Once we start to analyse the millions of stone ruins of southern Africa it becomes evident that the ancient builders had a very good knowledge of the cosmos themselves. One of the most compelling features of many of the larger stone ruins is that they are aligned with the cardinal points of Earth, solstices, equinoxes and most likely, Sirius, Orion, and other key stars. Johan Heine was the first real pioneer in this field who measured and analysed more ruins than anyone else, and by doing so, exposed the ancient skills of the FIRST architects.

Many ruins display very complex geometric forms and the knowledge of advanced geometry. This includes the Phi factor (Φ), or Golden Ratio of 1.618… which is the factor by which nature and space arranges itself. Examples of this divine plan can be seen in the shape of sea shells, pine cones, the proportion of the human body and all living matter on Earth or in the cosmos – even the way galaxies arrange

A spiral galaxy as an example showing how everything in nature conforms to the Golden Mean Spiral or Phi ratio of 1.618…

themselves. It is also referred to as the Golden Mean Spiral, and is linked to the free flow of energy in nature and the universe. Adam's Calendar is a prime example of this ancient knowledge by also being linked to the pyramids by a Golden Mean Spiral.

Many scholars have ascribed the construction of the stone ruins to the migrating hunter-gatherers and agrarians from the early Iron Age some 2,000 years ago, and later also the Bantu tribes from around the 18th century AD. No evidence can be found that these people built their structures with such precise alignments. This was certainly not the custom among the early settlers from the north, but rather something much more mysterious, left behind by a vanished ancient civilisation of the south – the ancestors of them all – the FIRST people.

When Cyril Hromnik wrote his masterpiece **Indo Africa** in 1981, he made many enemies with his outlandish suggestions that much of South Africa's current culture was influenced by Indians. His impeccable research in this area leaves little doubt that there was a large presence of Indian, Dravidian gold miners and merchants over an extended period as far back as 2000 years ago and possibly even earlier. They left behind an unmistakable range of influence which is evident in many aspects of South African culture and indigenous languages. Many of the stone ruins we have explored can be linked directly to the Dravidian culture, on which Hromnik has written many papers.

There are dozens of examples of shrines scattered throughout Mpumalanga and many of the stone ruins can be linked to Indian symbols and shapes.

Source: NASA

Above: The Milky Way galaxy, our home in the vast universe. Looking towards the centre of the galaxy we can clearly see the bright centre in the galactic bulge. It is the source of all kinds of energy and huge cosmic explosions that have a dramatic effect on solar systems and planets, including our own Sun and Earth. New scientific research indicates that such apocalyptic activity happens about every 5,200 years and causes mass extinctions on Earth, which gives rise to a new civilisation that has to start all over again. Such new civilisations have to try and figure out that they were not the first advanced people on this planet but were preceded by many others who lived very different lives in different social structures with different values.

Right: Chariot of the Dying Sun ruin. This ruin was studied in great detail by Dr Cyril Hromnik, who found detailed alignment to the movement of the sun, as intended by its Dravidian architects probably more than 1,000 years ago. It is possible that this structure was originally designed many thousands of years earlier by the FIRST people, who were the ancestors of all others on Earth, including the Indians. By the time the Dravidian Indians or Macomates arrived here some 2,000 years ago, they would have recognised many of the original symbols and structures, aligned to the same celestial bodies they were accustomed to. They simply needed to fine-tune the ruins for their own needs.

But it is important to point out that thousands of petroglyphs carved into rock, show that there is a link to people from other ancient cultures besides the Indians, especially the Sumerians and Egyptians.

The Dravidians left behind some important clues and even names that we still use in South Africa today. *"Until the 16th century the gold producing region of Mpumalanga was known as 'Komatiland'. Early Portuguese sources describe it as* **Terra dos Macomates**, *the land of the Komati people. Komati, was the professional name of a Dravidian merchant caste of South India. This name is still attached to the Komati River, Komatipoort, etc. During centuries of gold exploration they mixed with the indigenous Kung (Bushmen) creating the Quena (Otentottu), and with the Black people from the NW creating the aBantu people, and together they gave rise to the MaKomati. The pre-European form of the name was MaKomatidesa, Land of the MaKomati."* (Hromnik, 1995)

It is evident that many of the circular stone settlements we have explored are the remains of the Dravidians who were themselves obsessed with observing the movement of the sun and other celestial activities. Hromnik's detailed study of the 'Chariot of the Dying Sun' ruin near Carolina in Mpumalanga is a great example of this. Many alignments of monoliths, shrines and other marker-stones seem to be the work of these gold merchants from Asia.

But many other monoliths and alignments are not necessarily the work of this group. This follows our logic and argument, because there simply were not enough Indian/Dravidian miners in southern Africa to have built millions of stone structures. The original structures belong to a far more mysterious and a much earlier civilisation, whose foundations were covered by the sands of time and resurrected by the Dravidians many thousands of years later.

It seems to me that irrespective of the evidence that the earliest humans on Earth lived in this part of the world and developed the first art, first community, first mining, and the first cities on Earth, some scholars truly believe that southern Africa was a vacant piece of land with no history until the migration south of the settlers from the north, black and white. We need to remind ourselves that the first rule of archaeology is – civilisations build on top

of each other. Even in modern cities like London and Rome archaeologists are discovering older layers of their cities many metres below the surface, exposing a hidden past that has never been perceived before. For now, we can only imagine the mysteries of the lost civilisations that lie hidden below the layers of sand, scattered throughout southern Africa. But what caused those ancient cities to be covered by soil in such large numbers?

Top: The Chariot ruin. From our perspective this structure displays the same circular configurations consistent with harmonic resonant chambers and energy generating structures. The alignments to the sun were probably an important aspect of the design, but not necessarily the primary objective. The creation of energy seems to be the main design objective in most of the circular ruined structures.

Right: Johan Heine, measuring and decoding another stone ruin, to identify its celestial alignments and structural meaning.

Adam's Calendar

A graphic view of the central calendar stones at Adam's Calendar. The taller stone clearly shows its carved edge to allow the shadow of the setting sun on the winter solstice to reach the edge of the second flat stone.

Above & below: The stone altar about 700m north of Adam's Calendar. Various energy measurements and infra-red photography suggest that it is a grave. Many references in Sumerian tablets refer to Inanna and Dumuzi. They were the Sumerian Romeo and Juliet. We read that the Sumerian deity Dumuzi was buried in the deep ABZU, on the edge of a cliff on top of a mountain facing east, at his father's special place. This may yet become one of the most important historic discoveries that links human pre-history and so-called mythology to the 21st century. His father was the Sumerian deity Enki.

Adam's Calendar in 3D. All the calendar stones are dolerite, while the bedrock is black reef quartzite. It is the edge of what is known as the Transvaal escarpment. All the calendar monoliths were brought from some distance away to be shaped and erected.

Orions Belt monoliths

Horus stone

east

Credo Mutwa calls this the most sacred site on Earth, where heaven mated with mother Earth. He was initiated here in 1937. It is a well-known sacred site among Sangomas and Shamans. Many references in Sumerian tablets to Enki in the deep ABZU, or southern Africa, describe how he buildt himself a special place of observation, on the edge of a cliff, in line with his abode further north, which we believe was Great Zimbabwe, and the Great Pyramids in Egypt, which are referred to as the twin peaks. There is no other place that matches this description better than Adam's Calendar – a special place of observation. All the evidence leads us to this conclusion. On a more spiritual note, many psychics have told us independently that it is indeed a place built by Enki. On a television special that exposed sacred places in South Africa, a psychic exposed that this was the oldest place on Earth, and that it was built even before humans existed.

Above: The first ever statue of the Horus Hawk, made famous through Egyptology. This is just one of our irrefutable pieces of evidence that the Egyptians inherited much of their core symbols from the FIRST people in southern Africa. Note the broken nose or beak of the Horus bird lying flat on the side of the mountain. This statue is probably well over 200,000 years old. Our calculations of Orion's Belt alignments seem to be leaning in that direction.

South African Sphinx

*A recent discovery of the first ever carving of a Sphinx statue.
Standing proudly near the ritual path at Adam's Calendar.
Another crucial clue about the origins of the most important
symbols in human history and where they actually originated.
Not in Egypt or Sumeria, but right here in South Africa.*

Top: A good view of the ritual path at Adam's Calendar that joins the northern site to the main calendar site. The path runs among hundreds of fallen dolerite monoliths that all show signs of carving and shaping like the monolith in the picture above. A great example of unfinished work by ancient craftsmen.

Above: The Sphinx statue from a different angle.

Top left: A statue of Sumerian deity Inanna in the Paris museum, standing on two African gazelle, indicating her dominion over the ABZU.

Top right: One of the many Sumerian tablets that refer to Inanna in the ABZU. (source: Metropolitan Museum NY)

Bottom left: A headless statue along the ritual path at Adam's Calendar. It is possible that this was the first ever large statue of Inanna. The many references to her and her love for the ABZU (southern Africa) would suggest that this was a statue of this ancient Sumerian goddess.

Top: A view of Adam's Calendar (Enki's Calendar) from the south – perched on the edge of the cliff looking east towards the two pyramids and the rising sun on the Spring Equinox.

Right: The Skull stone. One of the many monoliths that show signs of severe erosion. Geologists agree that this kind of erosion would take many hundreds of thousands of years to occur. This one eroded much faster because it was part of the ritual initiation ceremony outlined to me by Credo Mutwa. The initiates were required to urinate on this stone. Nevertheless, erosions of the dolerite stones is a good indicator of the real age of the site.

Adam's Pyramids

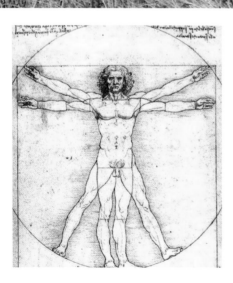

Architects and artists over the centuries, including architects of today, have copied their ancient ancestors by applying the Golden Mean Spiral into their grand modern constructions and art. Leonardo da Vinci's man in a circle 'Vitruvian Man' is one of the best examples of this and points directly to secret knowledge held by Leonardo himself. It seems that Dan Brown was spot on with his book the *'Da Vinci Code'*. When we think of pyramids,

we immediately imagine the spectacular pyramids of Giza, or the Mayan pyramids, that are built from giant blocks of stone and take our breath away each time we see them. But these are the exception to the rule. Most pyramids do not look like that. Hundreds of pyramids around the world are reduced to piles of rubble that simply approximate the shapes of a pyramids. This does not mean that they are not pyramids and most of the

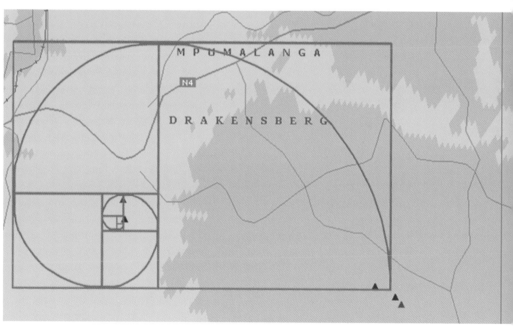

pyramids in Egypt are of the lesser category.

In 2008 we accidentally discovered two pyramids in the valley below Adam's Calendar. At first we could not believe our eyes and dismissed them as hills that simply look just like pyramids. But curiosity got the better of us when we realised that virtually every point at the calendar site is aligned or linked to the

Top: Adam's Pyramids as seen from the calendar site on the edge of the escarpment. They are about seven miles away in the Barberton impact crater, which is about 3 billion years old and is the home of the oldest rock formations on Earth. It may not be a coincidence that Sheba Gold Mine is about two kilometres away from the pyramids.

Bottom: A Golden Mean spiral perfectly links Adam's Calendar, the Stone Altar just north of it, and the two pyramids in the valley. This cannot be a coincidence. The odds against such an accidental structural arrangement is simply too high to even be considered. Because of this spiral, there can be no doubt that these structures were erected in their positions for very specific reasons which must include the flow of energy.

Johan Heine in 2003, clearly showing the pyramids in the distance shortly after he discovered the calendar. He began measuring and observing the movement of the sun. It took another seven years for us to notice the pyramids in the valley below perfectly aligned with Orion's rising.

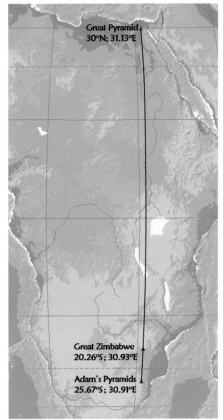

Great Pyramid
30°N; 31.13°E

Great Zimbabwe
20.26°S; 30.93°E

Adam's Pyramids
25.67°S; 30.91°E

A perfectly straight line along the 31 degree east longitude joins Adam's Pyramids, Great Zimbabwe, and the Great Pyramid of Giza. This can not conveniently be another coincidence as some would insist.

pyramids in some way. After all, the Egyptians built Sphinxes, Horus statues and pyramids. We had already discovered a Sphinx and a Horus statue, so why not pyramids?

After inspecting the mountainous outcrop lines in the valley we confirmed that the pyramid mounds are not part of the rock outcrop that caused concentric rings protruding from the centre of the impact crater. These two mounds are much larger, slightly out of line with the concentric bedrock, and they are perfectly aligned to the rise of Orion's Belt from the centre of Adam's Calendar. Some time prior to this we discovered that the Great Pyramid, Great Zimbabwe, and Adam's Calendar are all aligned along the 31 degree east longitudinal line. But Adam's Calendar is slightly out of line, to the left, if the line was drawn connecting the three sites from north to south.

Could it be that Adam's Calendar was somehow linked to the pyramids in the valley? I was convinced that there had to be a significant link between the two major points on the cliffs of the calendar and the pyramids some seven miles away, otherwise all this activity and construction along the cliff would have made very little sense to me. In hindsight, we should have guessed this immediately. The monoliths at the centre of Adam's Calendar; the stone altar north of it, and the pyramids, are perfectly connected by a Golden Mean Spiral. And so, it is not Adam's Calendar that is directly in line with the ruins at Great Zimbabwe and the Giza Pyramids, but rather the pyramids of Adam's Calendar that are perfectly aligned. It now seems that just like the Great Pyramid was said to have been the energy source of ancient Egypt, it seems that Adam's Pyramids were the energy source for the calendar and other sites not yet discovered.

Measurements

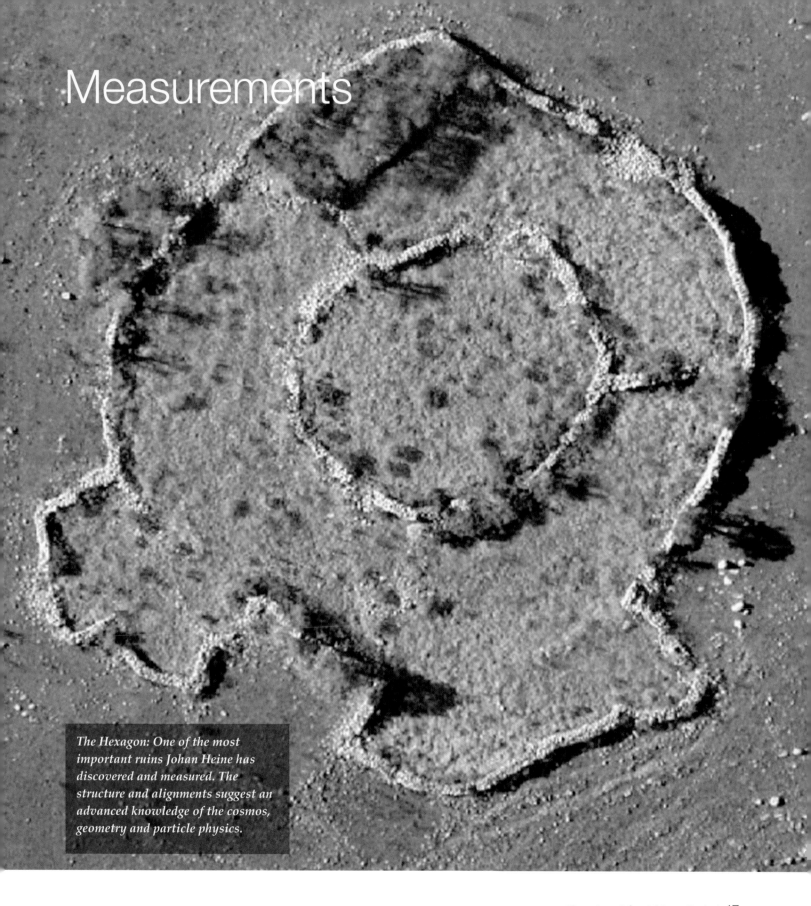

The Hexagon: One of the most important ruins Johan Heine has discovered and measured. The structure and alignments suggest an advanced knowledge of the cosmos, geometry and particle physics.

Right: We call this ruin the Hexagon. It is filled with the knowledge of sacred geometry, which was the ancient equivalent of quantum physics and particle physics and much more. It is moulded around the structure of a star tetrahedron, which is referred to by leading scientists as the fundamental structure of all matter in the universe. It is also synonymous with what the ancients called the fruit of life.

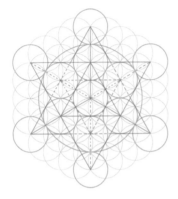

Above: A diagram of the fruit of life and its relationship to a star tetrahedron. But we can also see the continuous repetition of star tetrahedrons inwards. It is therefore a good example of infinity within a finite space in physics and geometry. Take note that the star of David is actually a flattened representation of a star tetrahedron, indicating ancient sacred knowledge. It is not really a religious symbol, which it became in later years for all the wrong reasons. Notice the 6 circles which surround the one in the centre – 6 around 1 – this is referred to as the creation event in sacred geometry.

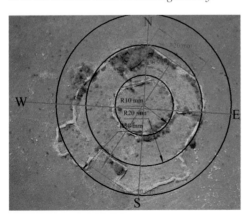

Left: The concentric circles in the structure indicate a knowledge of quantum physics and generation of energy through resonant chambers.

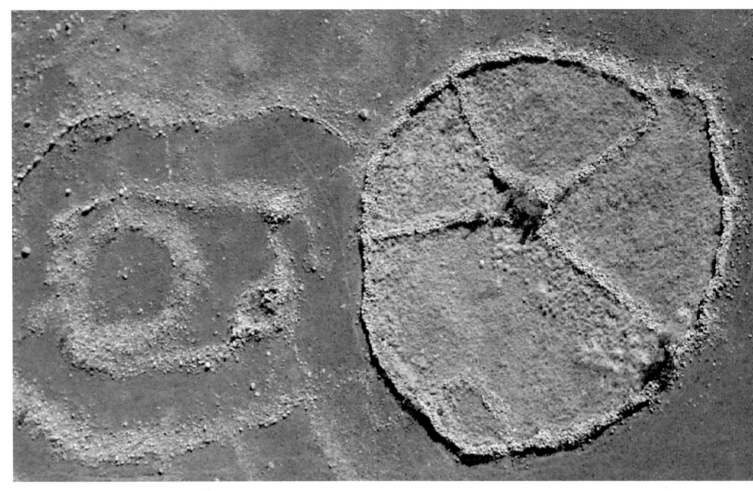

The Chromosome or Wagon Wheel is also clearly aligned to important cardinal points. But its relationship to the other ruined structures that surround it is even more impressive. The distinct horseshoe shape, or ohm shape (Ω), to the left clearly played an important role in its original function. The smaller circle inside the ohm leaves no doubt that sound was utilised for some purpose. The ohm shape is synonymous with sound and chanting. It suggests that this structure was important in the generation of sound frequency. There are many such ohm shape ruins scattered across the region.

Left: The Phi Factor ruin The outside wall has long gone but faint traces of it can still be seen to fit the large circle. This is probably the most complex of the ruins yet measured by Johan Heine. It shows advanced knowledge of geometry and is riddled with the Golden Mean ratio and Phi. It also supports the hexagon and star tetrahedron structure. We need to do much more work to get closer to understanding these complex designs. We cannot apply our current way of thinking to them. They originate from a completely different time and a civilisation that did not think the way we do today. It remains the biggest mystery in our human history.

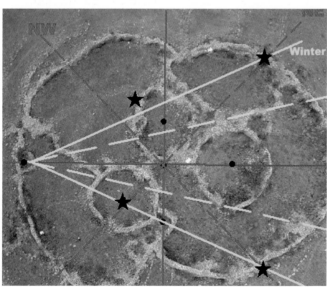

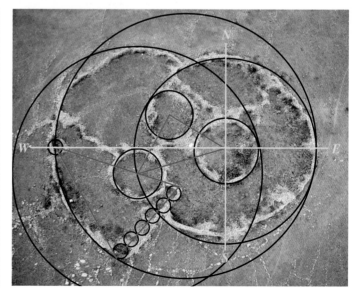

The Flood

Most people are familiar with the biblical flood. Some believe that it was just a story with no real relevance in human history. Well, this is not so. The great flood, or deluge, as it is referred to by historians, actually did happen. This event took place around 12,000 to 13,000 years ago, based on various archaeological discoveries. Many scholars attribute such an event to the rather sudden end of the last Ice Age, but there are many that claim the flood could not have happened because of the Ice Age.

Dr Paul LaViolette found evidence in core samples of polar ice, that there was such an event as far back as 14,500 years ago. But he also links his discoveries to the volatile nature of the galactic bulge, the centre of our galaxy, that produces vast regular supernova-like explosions. The intervals at which these central galactic explosions occur, correlate with what ancient civilisations called the appearance of the "Blue Star", which preceded the demise of civilisations. The Mayans believed that approximately 5,200 years constitutes an "age" of humanity, after which the people on Earth are destroyed to give rise to a new age. It seems possible that what the Mayans called the "five ages" was directly linked to LaViolette's discovery, which was also the cause of the great flood.

The Sumerian tablets give us a graphic description of the events that led to the great flood, which was also the trigger point for many advanced civilisations to suddenly emerge in many places around the world, and is consistent with the Mayan prophecies and LaViolette's work. We are told that the entire ice sheet layer that covered Antarctica slipped into the ocean, causing a spectacular cascade of gigantic waves pounding the whole planet. The waves would have been several kilometres high, travelling at close to 1,000 km per hour, like a ring of water around the planet, speeding from the South Pole towards the north, annihilating everything in its path. The cause of the sliding ice sheets was a large celestial body that entered the solar system and came so close to Earth's orbit that it caused huge geophysical disturbances. More than the Earth had experienced in human history. The gravitational effect on Earth was so large that it caused the glacial ice sheets, which were already weakened by the rising global temperatures, to slide into the oceans.

The countries closest to the source of the tidal waves would have been completely devastated. Especially South America, Australia, New Zealand, and southern Africa. While some ancient ruins on top of mountains remained standing, everything else would have been

Half way up a mountain near Lydenburg, a new road exposes three metres of sediment that shows stones from ruined walls and thousands of stone tools of the anomalous kind. A good argument for the flood theory, that destroyed the FIRST civilisation and covered their stone structures by soil.

overrun by the flood, and covered by soil and sand. That is why the largest majority of stone ruins, of the ancient civilisation of South Africa, lie below the soil, but remains visible to the trained eye. I believe that the structures we see today are those that were rebuilt in much smaller quantities by the survivors who re-seeded the post-deluvian civilisations that rose again after the flood. The evidence just cannot be dismissed as anything else. All the civilisations that emerged after the flood, did so with a whole new vigour and somehow they had all attained new knowledge. They all shared a common obsession to accumulate more gold than they had ever done before.

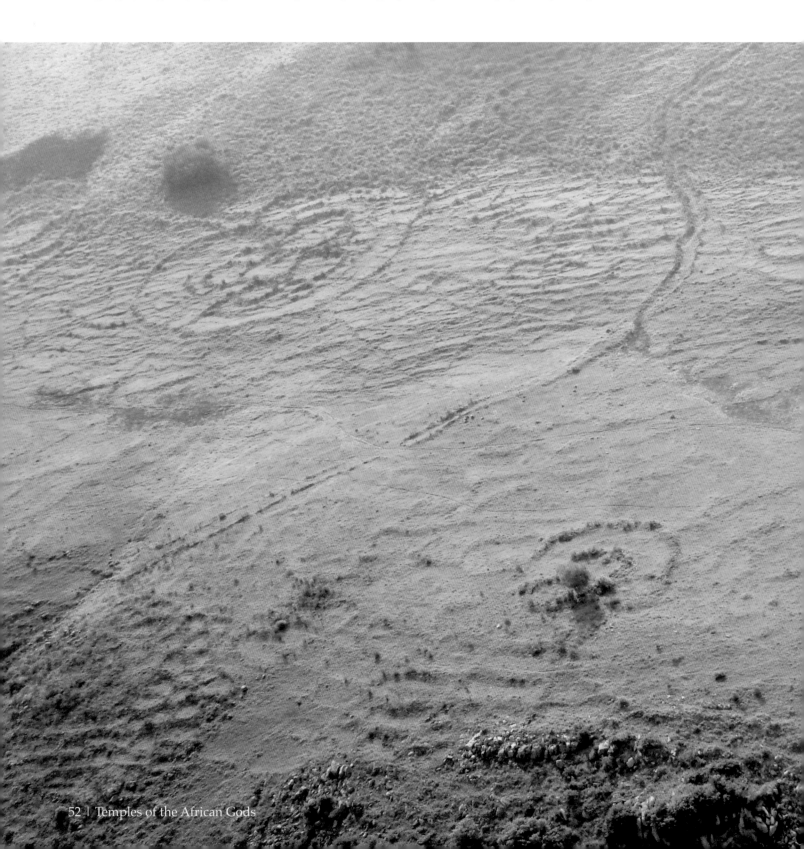

Lost Cities – Vanished Civilisations

Until recently, it was estimated that there are around 20,000 mysterious stone ruins scattered throughout southern Africa. This was a conclusion reached by Roger Summers in the early '70s after studying the work of earlier explorers like Bent, Dean, Hall and others who did excellent research and wrote several books about the ruins. In 1891 Theodore Bent estimated that about 4,000 ruins were scattered in this part of the world. Our own research of the past several years, which includes thousands of aerial photographs and hiking through hundreds of kilometres of mountainous terrain, physically exploring thousands of these stone structures, has shown that there are well over 100,000 of these mysterious stone ruins. This estimate was confirmed in January 2009 by Prof. Revil Mason, retired head of archaeology at the University of the Witwatersrand. Mason also suggested that there must have been an ancient population of well over a million people to have erected these structures.

The mystery deepens when we look at the extent and complexity of these ruins. These stone settlements are not merely scattered, isolated structures, or small clusters of stone remains – but rather large densely populated settlements and communities, linked by extensive agricultural terraces, all linked together by ancient roads that seem to stretch from Mozambique to Botswana and probably beyond. The extended ancient settlement that connects Waterval Boven, Machadodorp and Carolina covers an area much larger than Johannesburg today. While many have been destroyed by forestry, farming and road works, there are still breathtaking examples of these ruins with walls wider than two metres and three metres high. The entire area of ruins and terraces includes all the countries of southern Africa and covers more than 500,000 square kilometres.

But the latest scrutiny of the land using satellite technology reveals even more unbelievable results. No one could have been prepared for the staggering numbers of ruined structures we have discovered. The numbers are so large that they completely and utterly shatter any other previous ideas we may have had about the mysterious and vanished civilisations, our ancient past, and the magnificent lost cities of southern Africa.

Left: A great example of the complexity of these ancient cities. Showing circles, roads and terraces. One of the recurring curiosities is that many circles are built on steep slopes without entrances.

When you explore these ruins there is no suggestion at all that you are walking over extended sections of the circles. It is only from the air that you realise how the circles were all linked by a never-ending web of stone structures. So when you look at these aerial photos, look at the spaces between the circles. There in lies the real mystery of this vanished civilisation.

Many small circles, clustered together like a honeycomb, are still visible from the air. These will go a long way towards supporting the research by Ann Kritzinger from Zimbabwe University, showing these were not dwellings, animal pits, or storage silos, but rather leaching tanks for the processing and extraction of gold or other metals. The strange honeycomb structure also suggests that sound energy was used in erecting these structures so that they could harness the energy directly from the Earth – as demonstrated by Tesla in the late 19th century.

In nature many structures take on a hexagonal shape, because of its strength and fundamental link to the flow of energy. These ruins are clustered together in a very similar way. Did this help the flow of specific vibrational energy to help extract the gold? This kind of technique is not new to industry. Vibrational frequencies are used in many applications to separate substances.

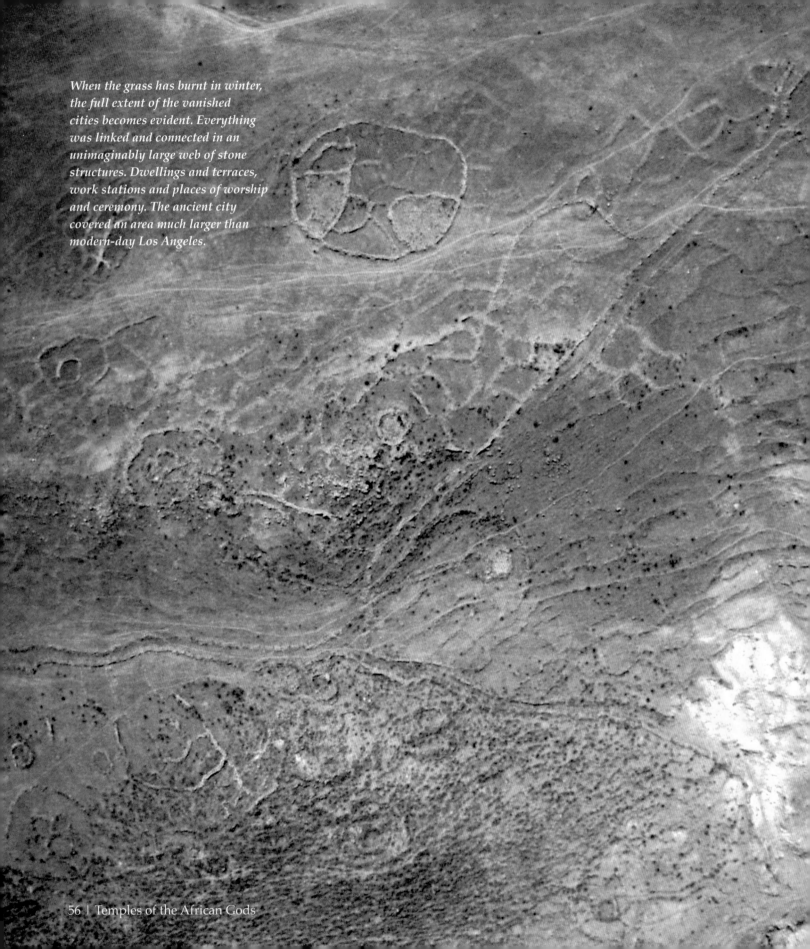

When the grass has burnt in winter, the full extent of the vanished cities becomes evident. Everything was linked and connected in an unimaginably large web of stone structures. Dwellings and terraces, work stations and places of worship and ceremony. The ancient city covered an area much larger than modern-day Los Angeles.

10 metres
Approximate Scale

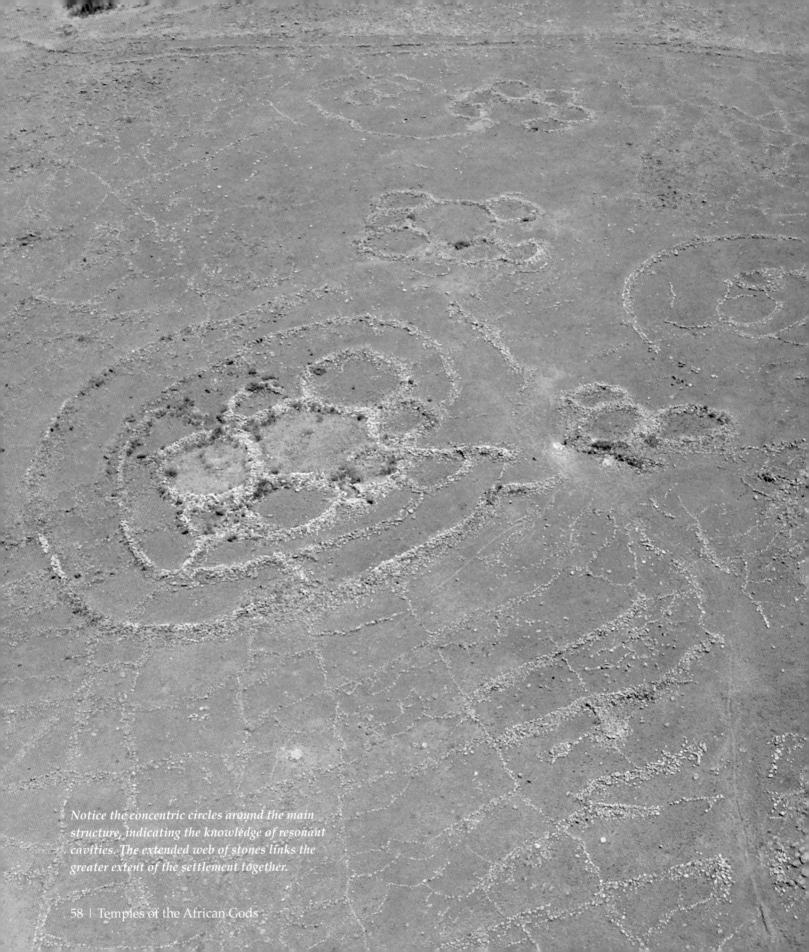

Notice the concentric circles around the main structure, indicating the knowledge of resonant cavities. The extended web of stones links the greater extent of the settlement together.

Once again – look at the spaces in between the obvious circles. A never ending web or energy grid that holds it all together.

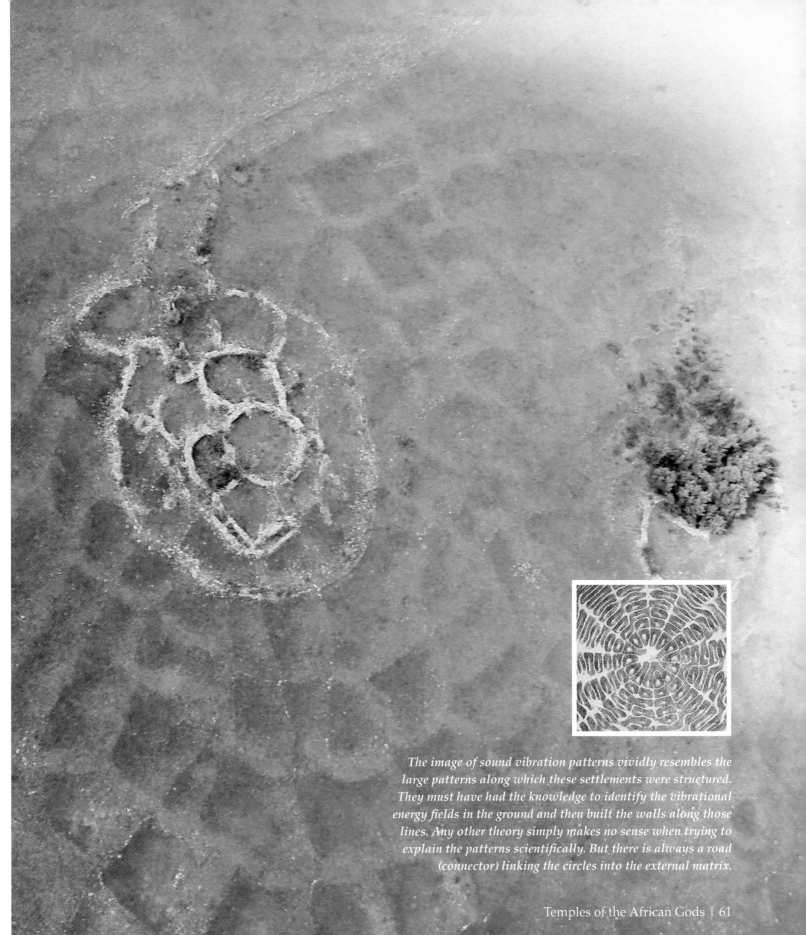

The image of sound vibration patterns vividly resembles the large patterns along which these settlements were structured. They must have had the knowledge to identify the vibrational energy fields in the ground and then built the walls along those lines. Any other theory simply makes no sense when trying to explain the patterns scientifically. But there is always a road (connector) linking the circles into the external matrix.

Calculating The Impossible

We mapped continuous settlements that cover thousands of square kilometres between South Africa, Botswana and Zimbabwe. We calculated the average number of circular structures per hectare; per square kilometre and the full extent of these settlements. Our immediate estimate was that there would be at least one million ruined stone structures. Obviously, our immediate response was what everyone would have thought; "that is impossible". But the calculations are even more staggering.

There are at least three densely populated areas or lost cities, each one stretching for about 100 x 100 km, covering about 10,000 square kilometres. To put this into perspective, each one of these areas is larger than modern-day Johannesburg or Los Angeles, for those who are less familiar with South Africa. We found an average 3,62 ruins per hectare. This adds up to 362 ruins per kilometre square; which eventually gives us the previously unimaginable number of 3,62 million stone ruins per one ancient city. The total number of ruins in all three lost cities adds up to 10,86 million circular stone ruins. I need to remind you that there are more "lost cities" out there, we have just not had the time to evaluate all of them yet.

Further calculations reveal the following:
For the purpose of our calculation we estimate that the original wall height was 2 metres – since it is still 3 metres high in some well preserved examples.

Average number of stones per square metre	30
Stones per depth of wall	5
Ave. number of stones per running metre of wall – 1m high	150
Number of stones per 2m high wall	300
Average length of wall in ave. stone circle	30
Total number of stones in average circle	9,000
Average weight per stone in kilogram	20
Average weight of stone in one circle – metric tonnes	180
Total number of stones in one lost city (32,58 billion)	32,580,000,000
Total weight of stones in one lost city (651 billion)	651,600,000,000

This new information forces us to re-evaluate what we thought we knew about the mysterious civilisations that once existed in southern Africa and its inhabitants that were responsible for building these large cities of the past.

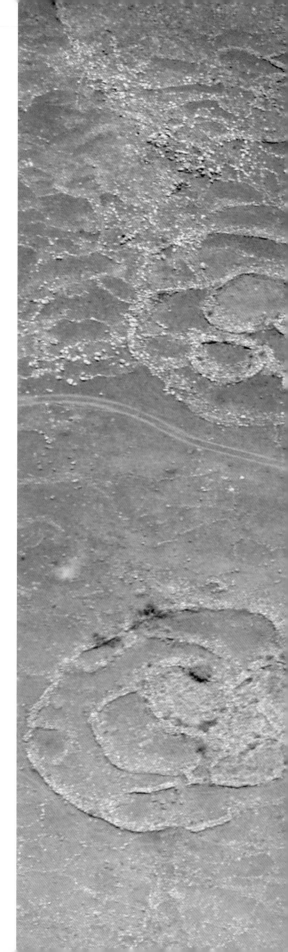

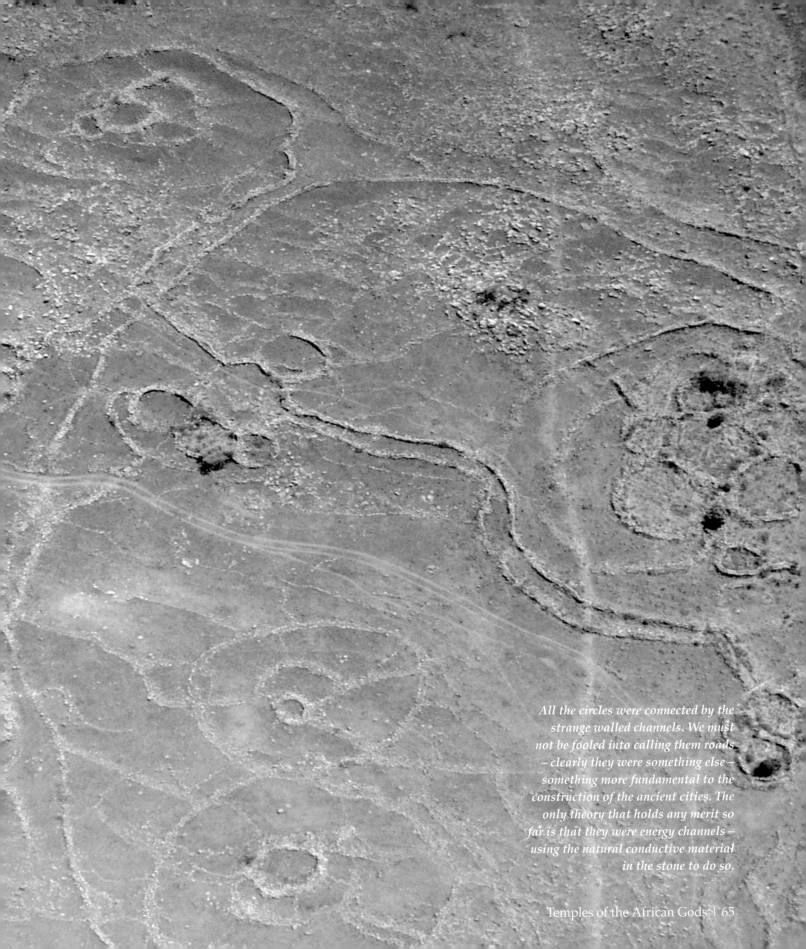

All the circles were connected by the strange walled channels. We must not be fooled into calling them roads – clearly they were something else – something more fundamental to the construction of the ancient cities. The only theory that holds any merit so far is that they were energy channels – using the natural conductive material in the stone to do so.

The first satellite images show a close-up view of the density of the lost cities. Even these images show the covered structures under the soil that once connected all of the stone circles.

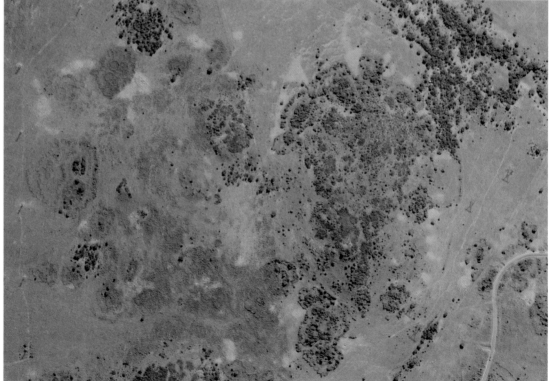

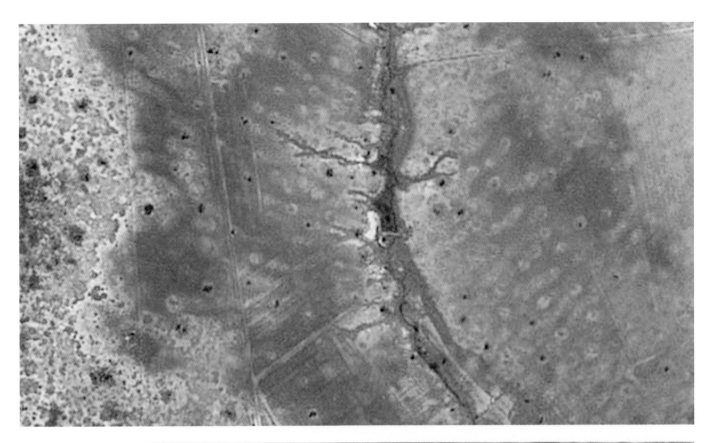

A view from a much higher elevation shows that the circles can even be seen under the soil in ploughed fields, where crops have been farmed for decades by modern farmers.

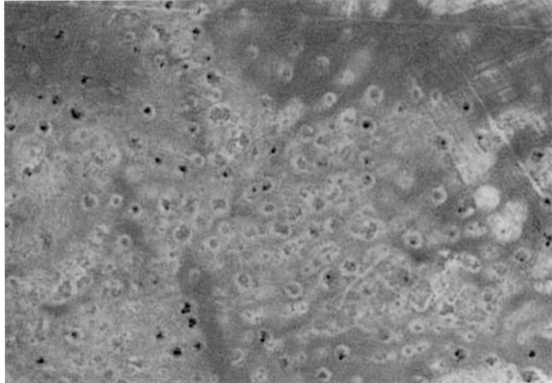

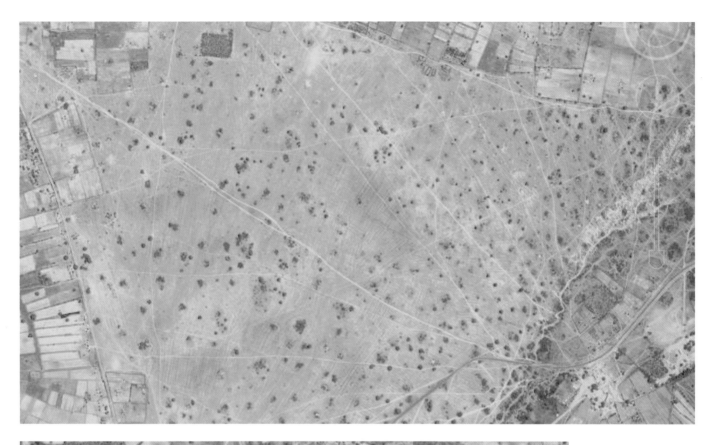

In the African bush, trees grow in clusters and in circular patterns around the wall remains. This becomes visible after becoming acclimatised to observing these patterns from satellite images over some time.

The Oldest Agricultural Terraces

Two roads join half way up a mountain and in the middle of an extended agricultural terrace. Some circles can be seen in among all of this. These terraces cover thousands of square kilometres. It defies any previous understanding about the ancient population numbers in southern Africa. Our latest research suggests that there was an ancient civilisation of many millions of people, who constructed millions of stone circles and needed all these terraces to survive.

It was reported by Summers in the '70s and others before him, that the ancient agricultural terraces in the then Rhodesia, cover about 190,000 square kilometres. This may at first sound a little outrageous, but when you start to explore the ruins across the border in South Africa, you realise that the ancient terraces continue in this part of the world, covering many more thousands of square kilometres. The meticulous construction of these terraces all lined with rock walls is staggering. Millions of large and small stones were used to construct terraces of different sizes. Many are built on very steep mountain slopes and the height of some terraces exceeds 3-5 metres.

All of the terraces are strategically placed around a water source on the mountain. Some of the gullies show scattered rock in a concentrated area around the stream which could be the possible remains of a dam that would have stored the water, which was then also possibly used for other purposes. Many of the terraces are sloped in such a way that would allow the water to move slowly with gravity, gradually from one level to the next. And there is not only one kind of terrace. We have clearly identified terraces that were used for grazing domesticated animals, and other terraces for cultivating crops.

How Old Are These Terraces?

In his book *Time Detectives,* Brian Fagan describes how botanists-archaeologists or archaeo-botanists excavated similar agricultural terraces in Peru and Egypt to analyse the ancient crops of the lands. Their discoveries were staggering, showing that the earliest crops in Egypt were planted as far back as 18,000 years ago and South America was not far behind. Sadly, such research on the ancient terraces in South Africa has not been performed, but initial archaeological analysis of some of these ancient terraces indicates that they could be older than 5,000 years. Once again we need to remind ourselves, that if this is in fact the 'cradle of humankind', and if this is where the first humans developed and began to grasp the concepts of art and survival, is it not possible that they could have grasped the art of cultivation long before the rest of the world? The sheer size of the lost civilisation and dates ascribed to these civilisations suggest that these are in fact the oldest and the first agricultural terraces on Earth – but much more scientific work needs to be done.

In 2003, archaeologists with the *Amapa Institute of Scientific and Technological Research* uncovered the impressive ruins of an ancient

This large rock near the top of a mountain at Waterval Boven, was once the water source for terraces below it, stretching all the way down to the Elands River. The rock is on the edge of a settlement of circles, which are now covered by trees. This was all destroyed, along with countless other ruins, by the road works when the N4 highway was built. We trust that the Roads Agency will become aware of this and start behaving responsibly towards preserving those ruins that have not been completely destroyed along the highways.

stone monolith observatory site at Macapa, near Brazil's border with French Guyana. This came as quite a shock to archaeologists as they did not expect such activity by ancient tribes in that part of the world. Mariana Petry Cabral, of the Amapa Institute said that "only a society with a complex culture could have built such a monument." These ruins are estimated to be 2,000 years old at a guess, but are probably much older. Large settlements that cover over 1,000 square kilometres, surrounded by terraces and roads, similar to the ones in South Africa, have been discovered deeper in the jungles of Brazil. It seems that there were ancient civilisations all over the world that are now causing archaeologists and historians to reconsider the activities of ancient man on planet Earth. But Africa remains the first.

Top: A spectacular view of ancient terraces and the complexity of their structure – against a steep slope towards the river.

Top: Once your eye gets tuned in, and you recognise the signs, you will see ancient terraces everywhere.

Left: This is what covered terraces look like under the trees. To most it will just be a strange outcrop of stones along the slope, but thousands of terraces lie hidden below the vegetation overgrown by trees just like this one.

Above & right: Stones from structures
and terraces roll down the mountain.
To the untrained eye it simply looks like
natural stones rolling down from the
mountain top.

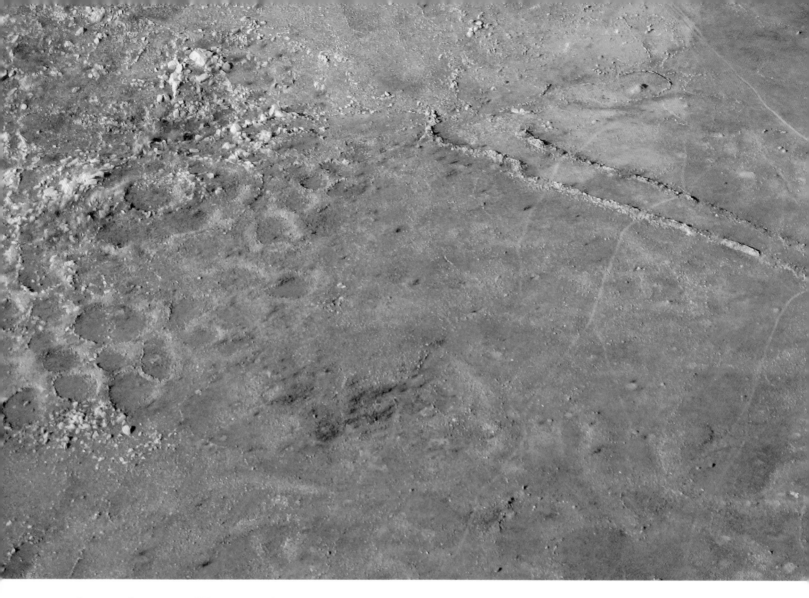

Ancient Roads & Mysterious Energy

Until you study the ruins from the air it is impossible to get a realistic idea of the size and scale of the settlements. While the walls that still stand above the ground attract our attention immediately, there seems to be a never-ending grid of walls that link them all together like a giant spider's web. This large and extended web of walls lies covered by the sand and cannot be seen or detected while walking among the ruins – this is an important bit of information to digest. We have found no record of any excavations or detailed research into this extended web of covered settlements.

It is also only from the air that you can identify the continuous ancient roads that link all these stone settlements. We have identified at least 500 kilometres of ancient roads that link these stone settlements. If these roads serviced this ancient civilisation effectively, they must have originally run all the way from the Mozambican coast to a number of destinations inland as far as Botswana and Zimbabwe and covered several thousand kilometres. More aerial

Photo: Gustav Janse van Rensburg – Rock & Rope

exploration will most likely expose the hidden roads that currently appear and disappear along the way.

For now we have traced the ancient roads from Barberton through Waterval Boven, to Carolina, Belfast, Middelburg, Bronkhorstspruit and past Rustenburg to Swartruggens into Botswana. It spreads out to the north, through Pietersburg into Zimbabwe. The well-preserved examples of the roads are always aligned by stone walls on both sides of the road. In some places these stone edges are more than 1.5 metres high. This remains the greatest mystery of the ancient roads. Why would anyone need to align all their roads and paths with walls consisting of millions of stones?

Based on our scrutiny of these ancient roads, we calculated that it required over 500 million large stones to build only the sections of the road that we have identified. This

Above: A stunning view of a road, or connecting channel, running through what was a dense settlement, now completely destroyed and covered by soil. It runs up a slope where it ends in the very distinct honeycomb remains of a very densely arranged structure. We believe that these were ancient leaching tanks for the processing and extraction of metals – most probably gold. (picture: Gustav van Rensburg)

A close up view of what the connecting channels or roads look like. Some places the walls are still 1.5m high. It does not take long to realise that these were not roads, but rather something far more important, that required a huge amount of labour and billions of stones to construct.

is an engineering feat of some magnitude and cannot be ascribed to migrating tribes from the north, who built paths for their cattle… as is often described by some academics. There is no civilisation in history who built all their roads aligned with walls. There is no documented record in history that outlines such a large scale construction of roads by the people in southern Africa. So who built these ancient roads? And when? And for what purpose? And what mode of transport did they use if the wheel only arrived in southern Africa with the Portuguese explorers in the late 1400s?

These roads appear and disappear in places and weave their way between the stone ruins and settlements. They seem to have connected all the structures in its original layout.

In some sections they run up very steep hills indicating that the road users had a very advanced way of transporting goods along these roads. And since it is not possible for horses or cattle to pull loaded wagons up such steep inclines, we have to contemplate a whole new theory for these roads, or channels. If they are not roads, what are they? And what purpose were they constructed for?

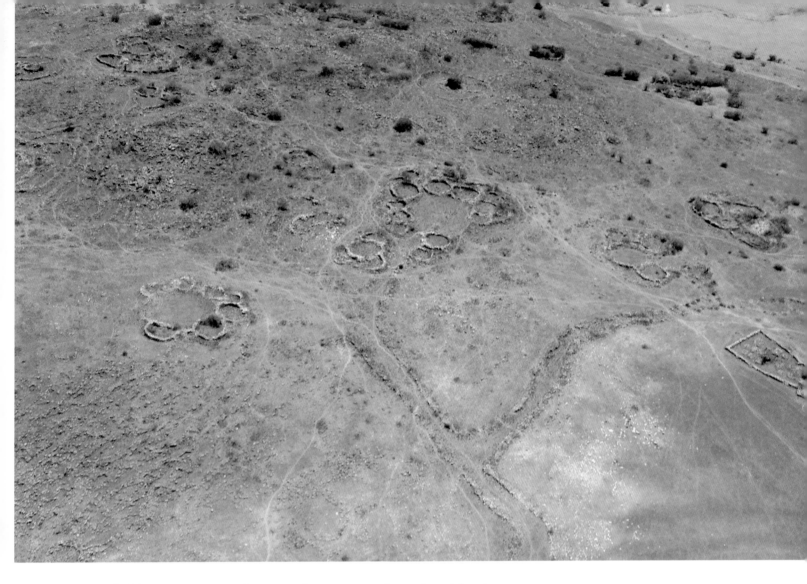

As laughable as it may sound to some, the first obvious technology that could be used on these roads would be some kind of levitation vehicle that somehow tapped into the magnetic content of the stones along the sides. The iron levels in the stones are very high and the conductive and magnetic properties may be the crucial clue that we must investigate. This levitation theory could be why the roads have continuous walls marking the edges. Very much like our modern trains run on electromagnetic tracks without any friction.

Top: This is a good example of how recent inhabitants used the stones to erect a more angular structure for their own needs. It is quite a common occurrence, that in the stone circle ruins, we find square structures, which were adapted by later civilisation.

Right: A short section of an ancient road (connecting channel) runs up a steep hill, right past more stone circles overgrown by trees. This channel was also destroyed by road works.

More examples of energy channels that were connected to the circles. It is feasible that the ancient civilisation used some kind of levitation device between the walls of the channel – in the same way that our modern trains float above their electromagnetic tracks.

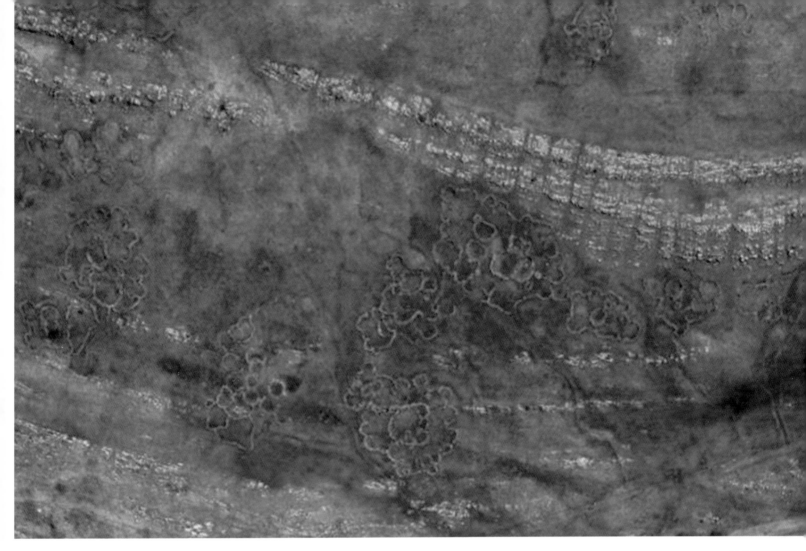

Top: These satellite pictures show the remains of intricate ruins at Bronkhorstspruit, South Africa. The short connecting channels link the ruins to the main channel bottom right of the picture. The spaces in between the ruins are not empty, but more ruins covered by soil.

Right: Michael Tellinger indicates the channel linking into a stone circle ruin. The channels often run into the centre of the circle, where they end with no exit possible, or no doors.

Above: A well preserved channel runs along a mountain top, with many stone circles that once linked to it with shorter channels.

Top right: A channel runs from a stone structure down a very steep hill where it ends at the river. If this civilisation understood the channelling of energy along these roads as we suggest, and if they were able to use the magnetic or other energy in the rocks to move transport vehicles via levitation, then they would have been able to draw water from the river up the steep hills to the stone circles. Many of the so-called roads go up very steep hills which defy any other mode of transport.

Bottom right: Another channel runs up a steep hill where it abruptly ends. It suggests that there was a stone circle which has since been completely destroyed.

Note the utter destruction of the ruins in the open spaces, around the stone circles.

The road/channel can still clearly be seen, but the circle it once ran into is almost completely destroyed.

Ancient Levitation Device & White Powder Of Gold

Before you call me crazy, let me quickly remind you of the most famous levitation device on Earth, and the most sought-after artefact in history; the biblical *Ark of the Covenant*. We are constantly reminded in the Bible that the Ark never touched the ground and that it always hovered several inches above the ground. From its construction of gold we can calculate that the Ark weighed between 3-4 tonnes. We are also told that it was carried by four men. This could obviously not be possible and therefore the four men must have pushed the levitating Ark as they walked.

Over the years there have been many speculations about the real content of the Ark, besides the fabled tablets of the Ten Commandments. Some researchers have suggested that 'Manna from Heaven' was a white powdery substance, which Moses fed to the Israelites in the morning, mixed with a little bit of dew. This white powdery substance has been identified by several scholars like Sir Lawrence Gardiner and David Hudson as "white powder of gold" or the "mono-atomic" form of gold. It is also called "The Philosopher's Stone, the Elixir of Life, and Star Fire" in mystic circles and by alchemists of the past.

Some leading science laboratories have done extensive research into this phenomenon and presented astonishing new scientific information that shatters all our pervious perceptions regarding life itself. David Hudson calls this mono-atomic form of gold "ORMEs" – Orbitally Rearranged Mono-atomic Elements. The study of the chemistry and physics of mono-atomic elements describes the characteristics of those elements which we know as the *Precious Metals*. These eight metals include ruthenium, rhodium, palladium, and silver (known as the 'light platinum group'), osmium, iridium, platinum, and gold (known as the 'heavy platinum group').

And just before you wonder what all this has to do with ancient ruins and the Bible and Moses and the Ark, let me remind you what Moses did when he came down from the mountain with the Ten Commandments. He took the golden calf and burnt it in the fire. He then transformed the golden calf, NOT into molten liquid gold, but into white powder. Then he took this powder, dissolved it in water and made the Israelites drink the water. Does this make any sense at all? Of course not – not until we discover the true properties of this white powder of gold, and then suddenly this mysterious part of our history books and the Bible makes a lot more sense.

The white fluffy, powdery substance, or manna from heaven, has the following properties. When exposed to a very small electrical charge it absorbs the energy and stores it. It behaves like a capacitor and energy storage device – not a conductor as some may think. It does however behave as a superconductor, conducting information instantly between one end and the other. Sir Lawrence Gardiner reported on experiments performed by European scientists to determine the effect of white powder of gold on human DNA strands. The powder also responds to tiny amounts of energy in a way that, when it is exposed to minute amounts of energy, it floats and defies the laws of gravity. Hudson reports that in the lab, when he brought his hand up below the flask, the low levels of energy in his hand caused the powder inside the flask to lift up and float.

Furthermore, the energised powder is reported to give off a bright, white, light previously not seen by humans. This is a single frequency white light and not the light that breaks up into the primary colours of the rainbow. And if you think this is all too much... wait... there is more.

The healing properties of the powder are most mysterious and this is most likely what Moses was doing in the desert. He was healing his people. The presence of the white light seems to repair all genetic defects in our DNA, and it heals human cells from any disease they may exhibit. This is most likely what Royal Raymond Rife discovered in 1931, when he reportedly found the "cure for all disease". A banquet was held in his honour on 20 November 1931 in Pasadena, USA, where 44 of the leading medical experts announced "the end to all disease". Sadly, this discovery was very quickly covered up by the pharmaceutical fraternity when they realised that this was a real discovery and would undoubtedly cause their demise. Rife is reported to have used a range of vibrational frequencies of sound and a specific frequency of "white light" to cure cancerous cells at will in his laboratory.

With this bit of information, it suddenly makes a whole lot of sense why Moses would have given this powder to his people. They could not have been a clean bunch, without water and sanitation in the desert for 40 years. They must have been full of disease and their minds were probably not very clear either. This "white powder of gold" has been a very well guarded secret for thousands of years among alchemists and healers of the past. Since the first gold mines on Earth were located in southern Africa, it would make sense that the early authorities, namely the gods or Anunnaki, under the leadership of Enki, would have used the advanced properties of gold to make life a little easier. It also explains how the ancients could have moved large stones weighing over 10 tonnes with relative ease, in their construction of Adam's Calendar and other megalithic sites.

The Ark would hiss and buzz and spark and shoot out long flames. No-one but the chosen few were

Ohio-state.edu

allowed near it and it had to be covered by a special cloak to contain its fury. It killed Aaron's two sons when they disobeyed a command and lifted the veil to have a closer look. For those that still find this a little far-fetched, let me remind you that the Ark was also used for a number of practical purposes by Joshua. He defeated several armies many times the size of his own army, by simply placing the Ark in their way; it brought down the walls of Jericho by using the energy inside as a resonant harmonic vibration to destabilise the walls; it parted the waters of the river Jordan; and it also parted the water of the Red Sea. This may come as a surprise to some, in which case I suggest you read your Bible properly, especially the book of Joshua, where it is made very clear that Moses was already in possession of the Ark when leaving Egypt. All of this was possible because the Ark contained the most precious and mysterious substance in all of human history. White powder of gold.

Shapes Of Ruins
As Energy Devices

The circular structure of all the ruins in ancient times suggests that there was a very specific reason for this. At first we are told that this is the simplest way to construct a building, but the truth may be a little bit more involved. The way that most of the stone circles in southern Africa are connected by paths and roads is very puzzling. From the air it looks just like a modern city with roads leading up to every driveway, but the main difference is that the ancient roads are lined with stone walls, still standing 1.5 metres high in places. It makes no sense why every ancient ruin would have required the road to run right into it.

One of the great puzzles of the stone circles is the absence of doors or entrances in many of the ruins. And where there are entrances, they seem to have been constructed by later inhabitants with different needs. In many places, at the point where the road meets the stone circle, there is no entrance, but rather a stone wall that meets the road. In some ruins, the road leads into the centre of the circular structure where it runs to a dead-end. This 'end' of the road is surrounded by a number of smaller circles, mostly without entrances, all of which are inside the large outside wall, often without any entrances itself.

Our current way of thinking delivers very few answers and only raises more mysterious questions. We simply cannot continue our conventional way of thinking about these structures and we will have to think out-of-the-box to solve this mystery. Nothing like this has ever been documented in history. There is simply no explanation why a large circular stone structure with a diameter of 25 to 150 metres, which contains a number of smaller circular stone structures, would be constructed without any entrances. But it gets even more weird – many of the internal stone circles also have no entrances and simply look like a cluster of grapes inside an outer wall.

Our first reaction to the ancient roads was obvious because we think in terms of what we know and experience today. Our first reaction was that they MUST be roads, because they remind us of roads and they seem to link all these ruins together.

But what if the lines of stone, otherwise described as roads, were actually something else? What if they were simply connection devices – connecting all the circles together? Because, when viewed from a different perspective, that is exactly what they are – connecting devices between all the circular structures. Those who know a little bit about electronics and the generation of energy will instantly see the similarity between many of the ruins' shapes and modern devices used in generating energy in laser technology and other advanced applications. The 'magnetron', which is used for generating vibrational frequency energy in many modern appliances like microwaves, is virtually a copy of many of the flower-shaped stone structures.

Some ruins still have the central monolith which can be compared to the central high frequency oscillator in the magnetron energy device. This central rod, or stone, is made to vibrate at a specific frequency which is amplified in the adjacent resonant chambers and then channelled out via the connectors that conduct the vibrational energy to another destination where it is used in many possible ways. The original vibration in the centre of the magnetron, or circle, can be generated by sound. The frequency or pitch of the sound will create the specific energy required to perform various tasks. These can vary from magnetism, to drilling, to levitation and many more. Pretty much what John Keely did in 1888.

Isn't it strange how we seem to rediscover ancient knowledge as we move into the future? Most, if not all, devices used to generate energy in modern times are circular or spherical. I suggest that this was also the case in ancient times before we lost such knowledge along with everything else that we rediscovered in the past century. The many patent drawings of Nicola Tesla outlining the generation and

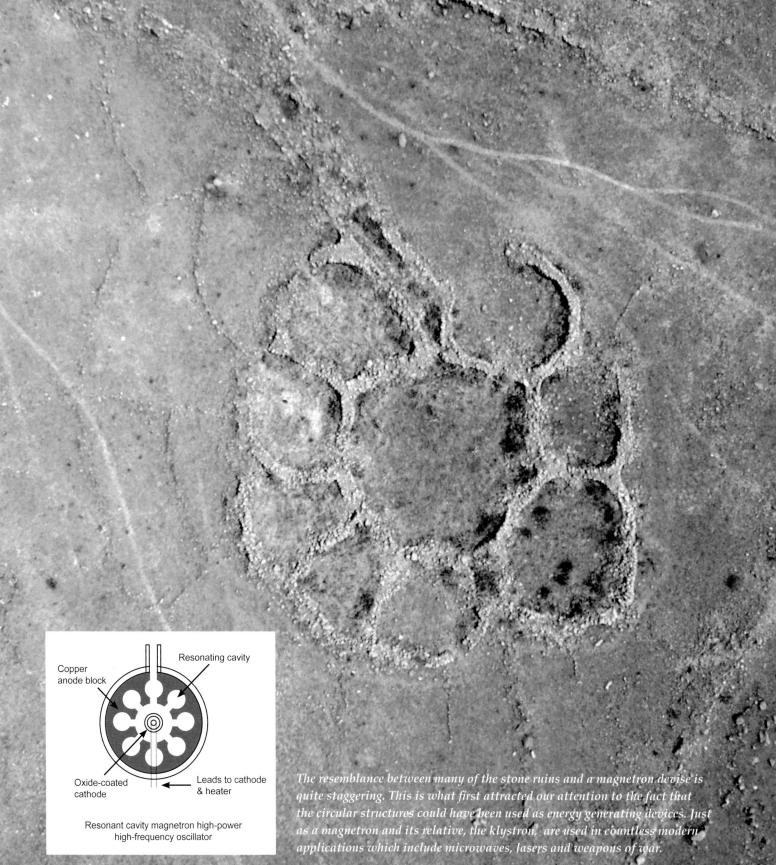

Copper
anode block

Resonating cavity

Oxide-coated
cathode

Leads to cathode
& heater

Resonant cavity magnetron high-power
high-frequency oscillator

The resemblance between many of the stone ruins and a magnetron devise is quite staggering. This is what first attracted our attention to the fact that the circular structures could have been used as energy generating devices. Just as a magnetron and its relative, the klystron, are used in countless modern applications which include microwaves, lasers and weapons of war.

The channels that connect right into the centre of the stone circles and make contact with one of the circular resonating cavities, makes it very clear that the architects of these structures knew exactly what they were doing. This indicates that they probably used the vibrational frequency of sound to generate energy, magnified it in the circular resonating chambers and then channelled it down the two stone-wall connector, to feed into the larger energy grid of the entire settlement.

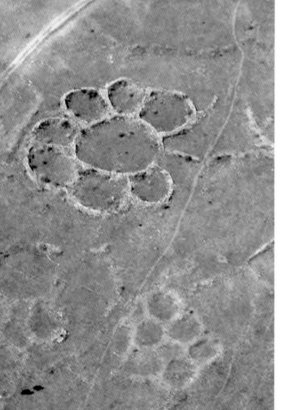

distribution of 'free energy' are also very similar in their circular structure to the stone circles of southern Africa. But stone circles are not unique to southern Africa, they have been found all over the world, in the most distant and unimaginable places – often in dense formations similar to those in southern Africa. One such example is the desert plain of northern Chile.

In his excellent book *'The Gods' Machines'*, that covers hundreds of ancient sites and structures from all over the world, researcher Wun Chok Bong shows in great detail how all these ancient structures were used as energy devices in some way or another. From Stonehenge to Avebury, these structures were not a simple assembly of stones to mark the rise of the sun on some arbitrary day – they were much more than that. Wung Chock Bong did not however include any of the stone ruins of southern Africa in his research, mainly because this is the most mysterious of all the lost civilisations on Earth, and secondly, because until recently, they were referred to as cattle kraals. But the energy creating principle is the only scientifically sound theory so far and is instantly applicable to the stone ruins of South Africa.

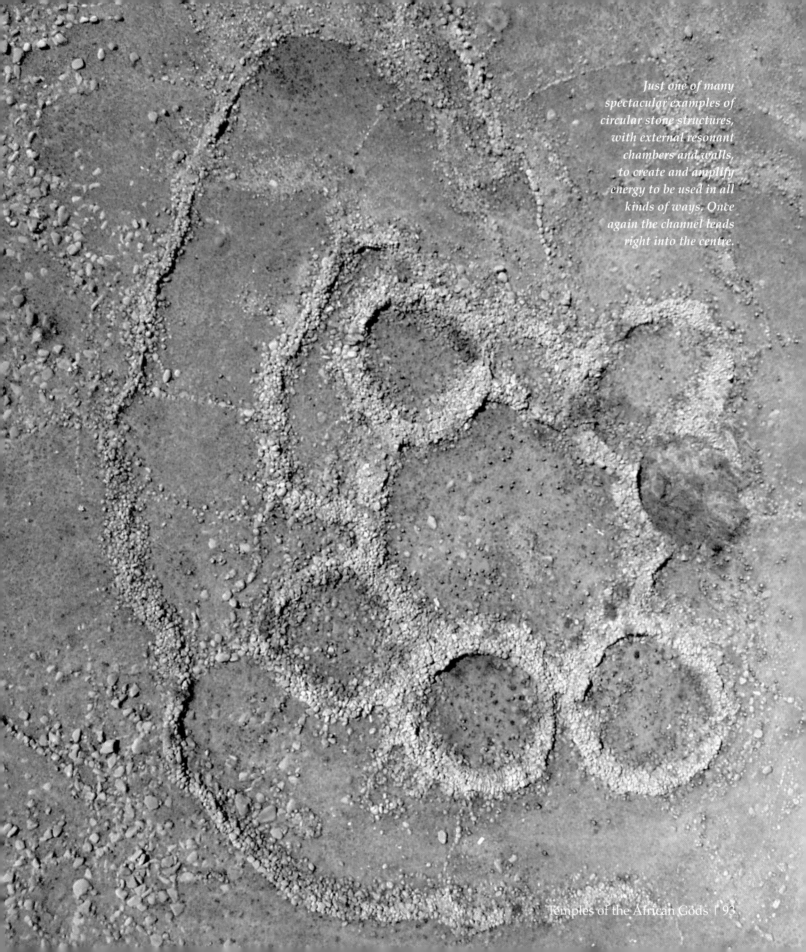

Just one of many spectacular examples of circular stone structures, with external resonant chambers and walls, to create and amplify energy to be used in all kinds of ways. Once again the channel leads right into the centre.

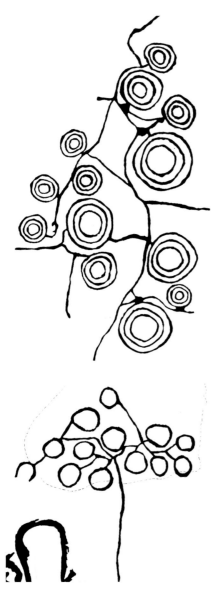

Above: These are archaeological sketches of stone ruins near the Nooitgedacht Dam. With our current understanding it is obvious that these are not stone dwellings from recent times. They look much more like resonant chambers for the generation of energy, most likely from sound. Some are more advanced showing 3 concentric walls for greater resonance and amplification. The roads can be seen as the wires that link them all together and channel the energy into the greater settlement grid.

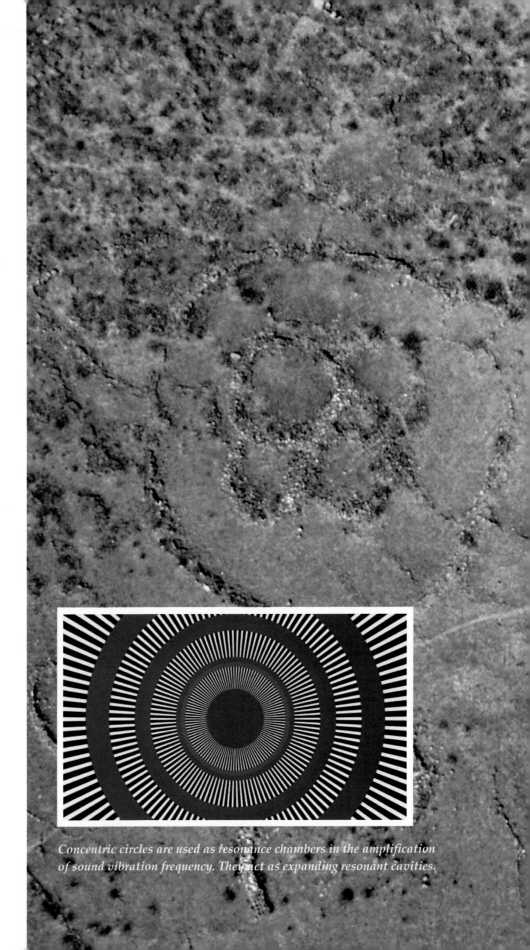

Concentric circles are used as resonance chambers in the amplification of sound vibration frequency. They act as expanding resonant cavities.

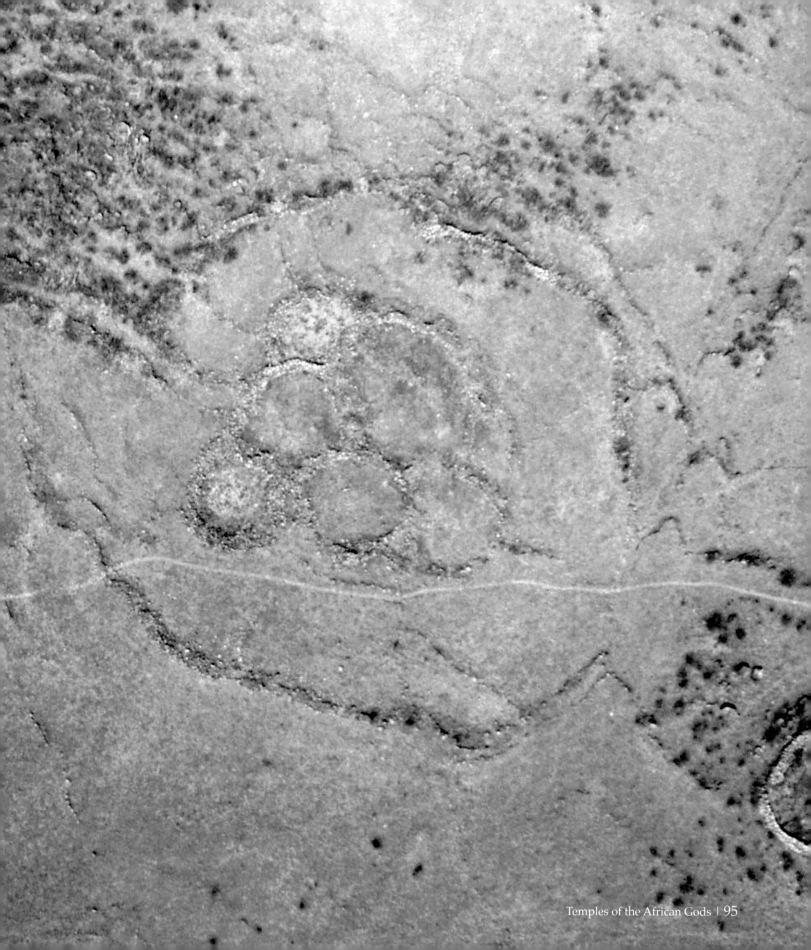

Population Mystery

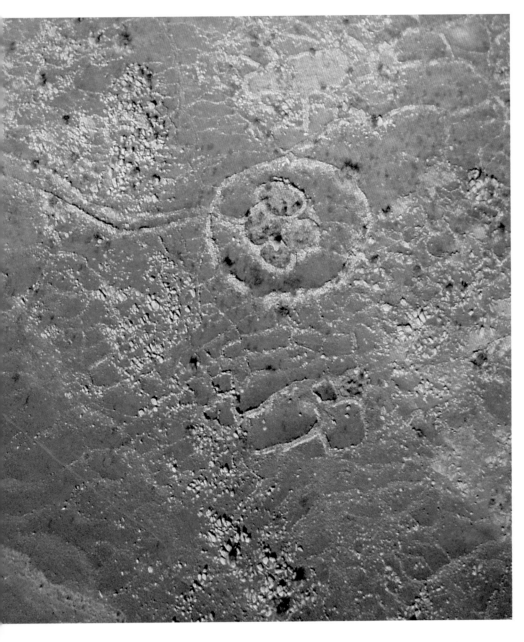

When we examine the southern African population models of the past 1000 years, it simply makes no sense. The estimated number of black South Africans during the time of the South African War in 1900 AD, was 800,000 people. The total estimated population of South Africa was no more than 1 million. The estimated population of the Basotho people during the time of establishing the kingdom of Lesotho in the early 1800s was around 20,000 people.

The current theory is that migrating tribes from north-east Africa would have moved in small individual groups of a few dozen at a time. The largest group would have been no more than around 300 people. These settlers would almost have behaved like hunter-gatherers, even though they built permanent settlements. They adopted a nomadic lifestyle, always ready to pack up and move in a short space of time because of wild animals, weather or other warring tribes. They certainly did not have the kind of labour force and tradition to build millions of stone circles consisting of billions of heavy rocks, complex stone calendars and roads that stretch for hundreds of kilometres.

When we ponder the large continuous distribution of stone settlements and terraces and ancient roads in southern Africa, which cover several hundred thousand square kilometres, it defies any logic. It raises a very important question. How many people must have lived here to need such a large expansive network of settlements?

YEAR AD	POPULATION
2000	45,000,000
1900	1,000,000
1800	300,000
1700	90,000
1600	27,000
1500	8,100
1400	2,430
1300	729
1200	219
1100	66
1000	20

Between the years 1900 and 2000 the South Africa population grew from 1 million to 45 million. This is a growth factor of 45, in 100 years. This means that in 1900 the population was only 2,22% of the population in 2000. Since accurate population statistics do not exist, let us use a simple extrapolation to arrive at some realistic numbers. For the sake of argument, let's be very generous and allow the population to decline by less than a factor of 45. Let's assume that the population shrinks by 70% every 100 years. The population model of South Africa would look like this for the past 1000 years.

It is obvious that there is something wrong with this picture. There must have been a time when the population was stable without growth for a long period of time. The survival rate of the inhabitants was low but somehow they must have kept going without becoming extinct. What this simple exercise does achieve is to point out that there must have been a stable population of indigenous and original inhabitants here that lasted many dozens of thousands of years. They were responsible for the cave art and rock art which includes paintings, beads and petroglyphs. Since none of the stone structures have been ascribed to the San or the Khoi people, it must have been constructed by the new settlers from the north.

It is obvious to any sober thinking person that the millions of stone structures that lie scattered throughout southern Africa could simply not have been built by those migrating settlers from the north, nor a handful of hunter-gatherers that may have lived here. This forces us to look for new answers and not allow us to be blinded by past perceptions.

Although we sometimes tend to deny it, South Africa is going through a highly politicised phase. While some of us are driven by strong pride in our own culture and unshakable faith in our ancestors, others have a strong tendency to correct the wrongs of the past with sometimes questionable actions. No matter what our individual liberal, political or historic views may be, the real ancient history of South Africa needs to be thoroughly examined. There were simply not enough people here between the 11th and 18th centuries AD, to build all these ruins and the infrastructure that surrounds them.

So who built these ancient structures? And when? And for what purpose? And why is there no documented evidence of such activity anywhere in our history? We should not be surprised that the Sumerians, the first apparent civilisation on Earth, give us very clear clues about what was going on in this part of the world thousands of years ago – long before any of us could have imagined.

From Stone Age To Iron Age

The roads through plantation forests are like archaeological digging sites. Many roads were dug right through the middle of stone settlements and they are filled with thousands of stone tools and strange anomalous objects. This is a short example of such a road. Virtually every stone shows evidence of being tampered with at some stage. The forestry trucks drive over the precious tools and artefacts not realising how important these places really are.

South Africa never ceases to provide spectacular evidence of ancient civilisations. In August 2009, University Of Cape Town doctorate student Kyle Brown announced a new discovery made at Pinnacle Point in the Western Cape province. The scientific online website '*Sciencemag*' puts it as such. *"The controlled use of fire was a breakthrough adaptation in human evolution. It first provided heat and light and later allowed the physical properties of materials to be manipulated for the production of ceramics and metals. The analysis of tools at multiple sites shows that the source stone materials were systematically manipulated with fire to improve their flaking properties. Heat treatment predominates among silcrete tools at ~72 thousand years ago (ka) and appears as early as 164 ka at Pinnacle Point, on the south coast of South Africa. Heat treatment demands a sophisticated knowledge of fire and an elevated cognitive ability and appears at roughly the same time as widespread evidence for symbolic behaviour."*

This vital bit of information goes a long way in supporting our discoveries, suggesting that ancient civilisations flourished in southern Africa in controlled communities and were much smarter than we had imagined. The large number of anomalous stone tools that we have discovered in the process of exploring the ancient stone ruins, is a simple testimony to this. Stone tools that have been shaped with the aid of fire, would have been a daily part of the chores and lives of the FIRST people of the south.

In 1997 a detailed archaeological survey was done of the area surrounding the Nooitgedacht Dam, where 63 stone structures were documented and sketched. The team went to a great deal of trouble to catalogue the structures and even recording the GPS points of each one. The report clearly states that based on the number of stone tools discovered in this area, it must have been inhabited for a very long time, stretching over 200,000 years. The most important part of this period would have been the Late Stone Age going back to about 40,000 years, which is most commonly ascribed to the San people, who were also responsible for much of the spectacular rock art in the area.

The researchers then continue to elaborate on the many circular stone structures, which they surveyed with accurate measurements and sketches, and then for no apparent reason, they claim that these structures were built by people in the Iron Age. They continue their report with a sketch of a single rock carving, that depicts what seems to be one

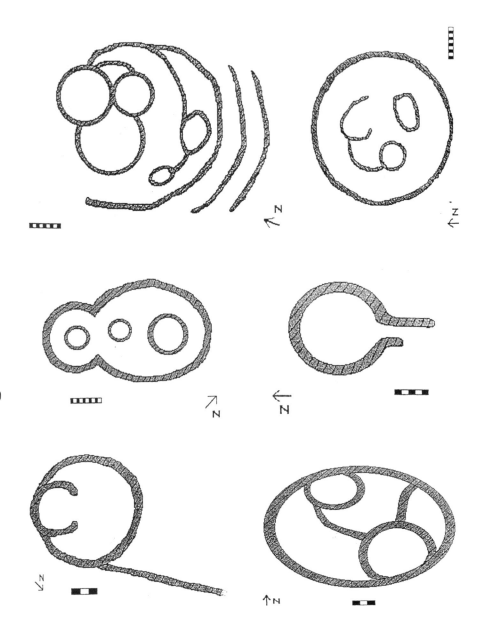

Above: A few archaeological sketches of so-called Iron Age dwellings. Everyone will immediately notice that these dwellings had no entrances. This is one of the recurring mysteries that some scholars just keep ignoring, and they keep insisting that these were dwellings. The shapes are consistent with our theory of resonant cavities for generating sound energy.

Left: A petroglyph near Carolina, South Africa, showing a strange configuration of circles and dots that are connected by lines. The crack through the carving is an indication of the age. It is our stance that the artists would not have made the carving on a cracked rock and especially not right over the crack. The erosion of the crack is probably well over 50,000 years old, which is an indication of the age of the carving itself.

Below: a sketch from 1997 of a similar carving nearby. The little dots on both examples are a real mystery. One theory is that these small piles of stone effected the resonant sound energy generated by the larger circular resonant cavities. They may have changed the frequency of the energy to a lower or higher frequency.

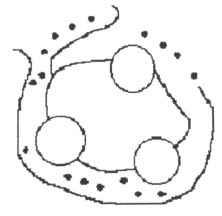

Far Left: A set of very sharp and pointed tools found about 10km south of Nelspruit, South Africa. Their tips are consistent with the kind of tools that could have carved the petroglyphs. When they broke, they were discarded, as could be the case with the tools to the right. The patina on these discarded tools suggests that they were not used for well over 50,000 years.

Count the circles. A view of the mountains near Rustenburg, South Africa. Just another small example of the continuous stone settlements that once covered the entire southern African region. The road channels that once connected them can only be seen on close inspection of the enlarged image.

A spectacular example of a dry stone walls near Waterval Boven, South Africa.

of the circular stone structures. For some unknown reason they report only 18 engravings in the area.

Johan Heine, Paul van Niekerk and I recently visited this area with the farmer Theunis Niewoudt and his son Ben, and photographed over 100 rock engravings or petroglyphs, which are mostly depictions of the circular stone structures scattered in the veld around them. One of the first things that struck me when looking at the archaeological report, was that neither the sketches of the

modern-day scholars, nor the ancient engravings, show any entrances to the stone structures. This applies to the outer walls and the internal circles. I would think that this is an unusual feature in any architectural drawing and should immediately raise many questions. How can you draw a plan of a building without any doors?

It is fascinating to note that the report does not mention this crucial information at all. But it is not only the carvings that do not have any entrances, the actual structures themselves

have no entrances. This is the case at thousands of stone ruins and has become one of the most perplexing mysteries of these structures. Personally, I cannot comprehend how this strange phenomenon has not caused a stampede among archaeologists to decode this mystery. Instead, this question always elicits some ridiculous reply.

People often try to impress others by throwing around words like "iron age" and "stone age" and other potentially confusing archaeological terms. Next time someone mentions "iron age" to

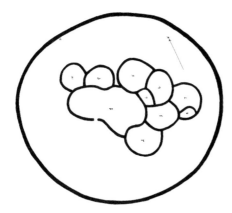

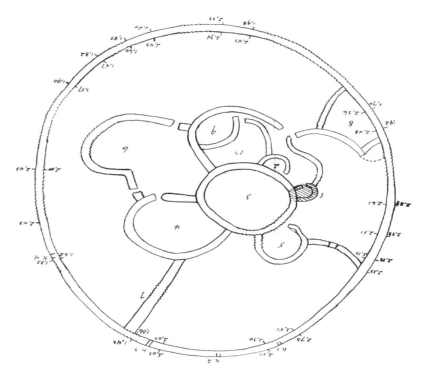

you, ask them… "which iron age are you referring to?"

The problem with the iron age is that the timeline varies dramatically in its appearance from place to place on Earth. Starting around 1500 BC in the Near East and Europe; around 1000 BC in the UK, and receding steadily as we move south to below the Zambezi River, where the current estimated arrival of iron production is between the year 0 and 100 AD. The term "early iron age" in South Africa is pinned at 100 – 900 AD. Various mysterious tribes like the "Lydenburg Culture" is linked to this era. In fact, the current assumptions of when the various iron ages emerged are also guilty of trying to force data to suit our theories.

But sometimes it just does not fit. According to the Bible, the first humans on Earth must have already had iron tools, since Adam, Cain and Abel used iron tools to work their fields. It also suggests that the first humans knew the art of agriculture.

Top right: Archaeological sketches of large stone ruins from 1939. The one on the left was the larger of the two which was completely destroyed by the building of the N4 highway. A great tragedy indeed. Once again the immediate curiosity that grabs our attention, is that there were no entrances in the original constructions.

Bottom: An aerial view of the ruin as it looks today.

The start of the bronze age is another problem. The conventional belief of when the use of bronze first emerged lies somewhere between 2000 and 2500 BC. This would have caused a big problem for the builders of the first Egyptian pyramids because they did not have metals hard enough to carve the giant stones. They did however have large supplies of copper and gold. We are told that they achieved all those marvels of construction with copper tools. We all know that copper and gold will not carve any stone. What becomes evident is that those so-called early primitive humans had a lust for gold long before they felt the need for the much harder and useful metals like bronze and iron. Does this make any sense to you?

This is what is written in history books about bronze and the curious obsession with gold. *"At the end of the Neolithic period, around 4000 years ago (2000 BC), there was a people who arrived in Britain that we now call 'Beaker', after the distinctive pottery that they were buried with. These people brought with them the skill and knowledge of producing and using bronze. Up to then, the only metal in use was gold, which is all right for decoration, but not hard enough for anything else. Bronze was a metal hard enough to hold an edge, and that meant a revolution in tools and weapons."*

Our teachers have always assumed that gold was used for decoration. This is a very naïve outlook and is made only by those who have not been exposed to the true properties of gold as a power and healing source. So, with all the gold in the world, it took another 1,000 years for iron to arrive in Britain. Can you see the immediate problem here? According to the conventional timeline of metals arriving in certain parts of the world, Stonehenge could not have been built before 2500 BC because they did not have metal tools hard enough to carve the stones. Once you start researching this phenomenon and you start to dig around a little, you soon realise that the mining of metals in southern Africa has a much earlier history, and the evidence is there to support it.

The Sumerian tablets tell us that the ancient people of the ABZU, or southern Africa were mining all kinds of minerals many thousands of years ago, long before conventional archaeology seems to suggest. I have accumulated many stone tool anomalies that were carved with metal tools. Archaeological evaluation suggests that these stone tools could be 50,000 years old or even much older. This poses a real problem for our current view of history, since humans were not supposed to

Left: A few examples of pointed stone tools. This is a very common shape of tools we keep finding virtually at every ruin.

have had any metal tools 50,000 years ago. Or did they?

In the spring of 2004 the **Edinburgh Geologist** magazine reprinted an earlier article on their website that relates to ancient mining in southern Africa. This is an extract from the article.

"When prospecting operations were carried out in 1957 in an area known as the Bomvu Ridge in the Ngwenya massif of Swaziland they estimated some 30,000,000 tons of iron with a mean value of 60% metallic iron content. The Swaziland Iron Ore Devolopment Corporation decided to mine the ore body and production started in 1964. The ore was taken by rail to the port of Maputo in Mozambique and from there shipped to Japan.

During the mining so many ancient stone tools were found that the news reached the archaeologist Professor Raymond Dart in South Africa. Dart sent a knowledgeable colleague called Adrien Boshier to investigate these finds and report back. What Boshier found was amazing, specialised stone tools made of dolerite, which is not a local stone, had been left behind by the early miners. These choppers, picks and hammerstones were not just on the surface but also deep underground. It seems that these early miners removed at least 1,200 tons of soft haematite ore rich in specularite from one particular mine, Lion Cavern, alone.

The question was how old were these mines? Archaeologist Peter Beaumont was producing evidence which suggested that these mines had been operated in the Iron Age, Late Stone Age and possibly even Middle Stone Age. However, hard evidence was still required in order to put a more precise date on the ancient mines. Then in 1967 charcoal nodules from some of the more ancient adits were sent to Yale and Groningen universities for Carbon 14 testing. The results that came back were astounding, dates of around 41,000 to 43,000 were obtained. Later from another early mine complex the buried skeleton of a child was dated at over 50,000 years." (**Edinburgh Geologist Magazine**)

Other archaeologists and anthropologists have suggested that these ancient mines must be much older simply based on the style of tools, artefacts and the presence of human remains. They have suggested a date of over 100,000 years. The signs are quite clear that iron ore has been mined for over 100,000 years in southern Africa but this information has been buried for some obscure reason. Could it be because it does not fit the theories of human evolution?

In 1973, **Reader's Digest** published a detailed article

Right: Perfectly carved holes in rocks. Many of these show metallic residue around the edges. As if they were used as crucibles for molten metals.

Top: A larger cavity in a rock with distinct metallic residue around the rim of the hollowed section. We have found several such examples.

Below: Strange stone tool/object found inside a stone circle ruin near Koster, South Africa.

Bottom: A strange tool found on a terrace near Waterval Boven. Estimated to be at least 50,000 years old.

about the ancient mines in southern Africa. This is a short extract to further highlight these ancient mines.

"Beaumont was engaged to explore the site with Boshier. In 18 months the young researchers located ten ancient filled-in pits, some as deep as 45 feet, from which a bright-red ore called hematite had been dug. In these pits were some of the richest deposits of Stone Age relics ever uncovered, including thousands of cleavers, picks, hammers, wedges and chisels, heavily bruised from use. From archaeological and geologic evidence, the earliest strata have been estimated to be 70,000 to 80,000 years old. . .

Having discovered the reason for the mines, Boshier and Beaumont began to look for the miners. It was this quest that led them to start digging at Border Cave. The cave had been investigated in 1934, and scientists had found various pieces of fossilized human skull and bone there, including the infant skeleton lying in a shallow grave in a Middle Stone Age stratum. But since radiocarbon dating had not yet been developed and the bones were of modern type, they evoked little interest. The earth of the grotto had remained undisturbed for 30 years when Boshier and Beaumont plunged their trowels into it in December 1970. In 50 active days, before supplies and money ran out, they unearthed some 300,000 artefacts and charred animal bones, many of creatures long extinct. Charcoal from an overlying ash level, more recent than the stratum in which the child's skeleton was discovered, proved to exceed the limit of radiocarbon dating, which is around 50,000 years. Thus the burial had occurred more than 50,000 years ago, but exactly how much earlier is difficult to say. Stone implements and ground ochre appear right down to bedrock, nine feet below the surface, suggesting that the cavern had been occupied for the last 100,000 years. 'Practically everything we found was three times older than the books said it should have been,' Boshier observes."(**Reader's Digest**)

It is commonly believed that people in the early and middle Stone Age did not build circular stone structures. This is also a misconception. If only they took the time to excavate the well-known site of Melville Koppies, Johannesburg, they may be surprised to find that the foundations were originally laid by Stone Age settlers. In Wolmeransstad we discovered Stone Age tools in an ancient circular stone ruin, which is part

of a larger stone settlement. There is also evidence of pathways or roads connecting some of these structures. The incredible thing is that the stone axes from these stone ruins have been dated to be between 200,000 and 400,000 years old. In the same settlement we found the remains of mud hut walls that cannot be older than 300 years. This simply indicates how civilisations build on top of each other or simply re-inhabit existing structures. At this particular site there is overwhelming evidence of continued human habitation for several hundred thousand years. Near Rustenburg there are stone ruins that have been estimated to be about 18,000 years old, and which display signs of agriculture and the probable presence of an extinct domesticated animal called the fat-tailed sheep. The same can be said for the ruins at Waterval Boven, where Stone Age tools dating to way over 200,000 years ago have been found near pottery dating to around the 1600's.

In the same *Reader's Digest* article, Boshier and Beaumont continue with the following statement.

"…as early as 100,000 years ago man had developed an interest in happenings beyond the needs of survival. He had begun to question the purpose of existence and the nature of human destiny, to seek causes and fabricate explanations. This was the birth of intellect and the ascendancy of reason.'. . . It may be years before prehistorians can fully evaluate the significance of these. . . discoveries, but from the evidence it seems clear that modern man evolved on earth far earlier than has been realized and that most probably it was in the darkness of an African cave that the miracle of civilization had its genesis."

So what was going on here for so long? What was the main attraction that kept people so busy, in this part of the world, for several hundred thousand years? GOLD!

Picture: Brenda Sullivan

Top: The largest grind stone we have found to date. About 1.5m long and close to a metre wide. Tools like these should be smooth on the inside grinding surface. The erosion patterns inside this one, suggest that it has not been used for well over 100,000 years.

Bottom: Holes carved in a flat triangular rock are not just random holes but could well be an intricate sundial as indicated by Brenda Sullivan.

Quest For Gold

One of dozens of gold mines that I visited with Marius Brits near Lydenburg, South Africa. The current belief is that they were first mined during the 1880s gold rush. We have a very different take on this tale. It is no coincidence that wherever you find old gold mines, there are always remains of ancient stone circles, terraces and signs of lost civilisations, who mined gold here long before anyone else. It is more likely that the prospectors in the late 1800s found the ancient gold mines near the stone circles and realised that wherever there are circles, there is gold. A good argument for this is that many of these mines are high up against the mountains, near stone circles. Not the normal place you would find gold mines.

When Fernandes left the port of Sofala, Mozambique in 1510 AD, his instructions were clear and simple – find the kings of the fabled Monomotapa and find the gold of the land. Since then, the scramble for Africa by the colonialists has pretty much revolved around gold and other precious minerals in the ground. Somehow the ancient inhabitants in Africa knew how to extract gold, and have been doing so for thousands of years. The learned Moors who tried to make sense of the ruins in Zimbabwe around 1552, believed that the stone structures were "very ancient" and were constructed to keep control and possession of the gold mines. Gold seems to be the continuous common denominator in all of human history, and it seems to have started right here in southern Africa. Thousands of ancient gold mines have been reported over the past few centuries and we have identified several dozen ourselves.

But the Portuguese were beaten to the gold rush by a few others before them. Egyptian pharaoh Rameses the Great, around 1300 BC, is said to have crossed the African continent to the southern tip, in search of gold, and then sailed beyond to Antarctica. Roman emperor Antoninus Pius controlled gold digging operations here in 138 AD. Arab records show that Arabic traders were already doing trade with southern Africa since around 800 AD. And let's not forget the Indian gold merchants, the MaKomates, who traded gold from southern Africa, possibly as far back as 2000 BC.

If the Sumerian texts are correct in their description of ancient gold mines in southern Africa as far back as 280,000 years ago, it makes absolutely perfect sense as to where King Solomon got all his gold from. Because by the time he came to power he must have obtained his gold from a place with a long and established history of gold mining. Solomon lived around 1000 BC and according to texts, accumulated more wealth than any other king before him. The mysterious biblical Land of Ophir, takes on a whole new meaning and there can be no doubt where most of the gold came from in those early days. This is after all the place where most of the gold in the world has been mined in modern history, and it was no different in ancient times.

Is it a coincidence that arguably the richest gold mine in the world today, Sheba Gold Mine, is located right here, a few miles from Adam's Calendar, in Mpumalanga, South Africa? These may seem like naïve questions to some, but after witnessing the enormous ancient cities and civilisations in southern Africa myself, I am convinced that what we think we know about our ancient human history is further from the truth than we have ever imagined. It is also important to note that the word 'Ophir' stems from the ancient near-eastern name for Africa which was 'Afir' or 'Aphir'. This later led to the people of Africa being referred to as "K'Afir" and we all know where this expression led to. Right next to Sheba Gold Mine, we recently discovered three ancient gold mines, one of them being probably over 100 metres deep. These lie right on the edge of a completely ruined stone settlement, which covers the entire hill.

Above: This Roman coin of Antoninus Pius who ruled Rome from 138AD was found by Theodore Bent about 25m deep in a gold mine near Mutare, Zimbabwe. A crucial bit of information that was conveniently misplaced. The Romans were here mining gold or trading in gold at the same time as the Indian Dravidians.

Top: Terraces, and at least 8 stone circles near Lydenburg, covered by soil and grass, only in this small section of the mountain, surrounded by hundreds of ancient gold mines that were re-used by the prospectors of the 1800s. Once they knew that the ancient mines were associated with the circles, it became a stampede to find the next ancient mine and claim it.

Left: Some of the mines were barricaded by the last miners to prevent scavengers dipping into their golden ore. It does not seem that it really worked.

Top left: A few more examples of the dozens of deserted mines high up against the mountain.

Top right: Michael Tellinger shows the proportions of the mine tunnel. It was not a pleasant task to cart the ore out of there. Notice the Orbs floating around Michael – Souls of the dead miners or new inquisitive ones feeding on the energy of the past?

Bottom right: Another mine entrance with unknown depth.

Examples of 2 well preserved stone circles. The larger one has several large stones built into the walls. We do not have any theories on this as yet. But based on the high content of quartz it could have aided in the process of conducting and generating energy.

Top: The remains of the hoist house from the late 1800s mining activities. A cable ran down to the valley near the river where the ore was crushed and processed.

Right: A spectacular picture of a mine shaft filled with so many Orbs that we can hardly see the passage. For those who are new to the Orb phenomenon – these are non-physical energies in spherical form and many different sizes. Some believe that they are souls in a non- physical form. There has been some research done on the spheres and actual energy readings were measured. Orbs cannot be seen with the naked eye, but digital cameras pick them up because of their ability to capture infra-red and ultra-violet parts of the light spectrum. Some children and adults can however see Orbs with the naked eye. This could be evidence of retinal evolution taking place, or simply the rise of consciousness.

Two great examples of ancient gold mines going straight down into the ground. The holes are very deep, probably more than 100m. There are no records of these mines and somehow they slipped through the fingers of the mining giants. Not surprisingly, they are close to the richest gold mine in the world today - Sheba Gold Mine.

Above & left: A road cuts right through the centre of a stone circle. The strata is spectacular – showing all kinds of anomalous tools, and even ash from unknown activity.

Above: Five-metre high strata along a road shows sediment and deposits of stones and monoliths from stone walls of ancient ruins.

Above: Just one of thousands of anomalous tools washed into the road high up against the mountain.

Top: Michael Tellinger sits dangerously close to the edge of a deep mine shaft.

Left: A snap shot of the shaft itself. It is probably over 100m deep and it may even have side shafts splitting away from the main vertical.

Top: Johan Heine examines the entrance to an ancient gold mine high on a mountain in Mpumalanga, South Africa.

Left: Strangely shaped and carved stones lie scattered among the many stone circles that surround the mine shaft.

Right: Michael Tellinger points out the remains of a stone circle wall, which was part of a large settlement all around the deep mine shaft. Note the distinct shape of one of Adam's Pyramids in the background. Always close to the gold – in antiquity and in modern times too.

Sumerian Tablets

In 2004 the *National Geographic News* website posted this item about the Sumerians.

"The people known as Sumerians are credited with starting the first civilization and building the first settlements worthy of being called cities. They also invented writing, and then they wrote and wrote and wrote, filling millions of tablets with their intricate, detailed characters. They left behind everything from religious texts to poetry to receipts, much of which remains preserved 5,000 years later. The Sumerians settled and farmed the area between the Tigris and Euphrates Rivers in Mesopotamia, now part of Iraq. Around 3500 B.C., they became the first people on Earth to congregate in cities, to use complex mathematics, and to record their ideas with a written language. They did most of their writing between 3000 and 2000 B.C. Over the next millennium, they were gradually assimilated into the Babylonian civilization, which continued to advance Sumerian literature, astronomy, and mathematics."

For people who study religious texts, it is critical to note that much of what we read in the Bible has been taken and adapted from thousands of Sumerian clay tablets. These tablets have slowly and systematically been deciphered over the past 150 years by a growing number of scholars. Today, some universities have established Sumerian translation departments and employ advanced computer programs to scan and translate these clay tablets. It was only in the past 40 years however, that the true meaning of these translations started to play havoc with our perception of human history. It is commonly accepted by scholars across the board that we have inherited

This is MS 2855 of the Schoyen Collection in the Oslo museum. One of the most important Sumerian tablets in existence. It is one of six clay tablets in different museums of the world that actually name the pre-flood kings who ruled the world over a total period of 222,600 years. Two of them give exactly the same information while the others have slight deviations. The actual translations is this:

LIST OF KINGS AND CITIES FROM BEFORE THE FLOOD IN ERIDU: ALULIM RULED AS KING 28,800 YEARS. ELALGAR RULED 43,200 YEARS. ERIDU WAS ABANDONED. KINGSHIP WAS TAKEN TO BAD-TIBIRA. AMMILU'ANNA THE KING RULED 36,000 YEARS. ENMEGALANNA RULED 28,800 YEARS. DUMUZI RULED 28,800 YEARS. BAD-TIBIRA WAS ABANDONED. KINGSHIP WAS TAKEN TO LARAK. EN-SIPA-ZI-ANNA RULED 13,800 YEARS. LARAK WAS ABANDONED. KINGSHIP WAS TAKEN TO SIPPAR. MEDURANKI RULED 7,200 YEARS. SIPPAR WAS ABANDONED. KINGSHIP WAS TAKEN TO SHURUPPAK. UBUR-TUTU RULED 36,000 YEARS. TOTAL: 8 KINGS, THEIR YEARS: 222,600

almost everything we know from the Sumerians. The wheel, writing, medicine, astronomy, architecture, agriculture, geometry, mathematics, the law, and much more. It was the crafty Sumerians who first developed and applied these disciplines. This early civilisation also had their pantheon of 12 gods who ruled their lives, rewarded them and punished them if they stepped out of line. This is where the first Holy Trinity originated between the gods Anu, Enlil and Enki.

The Sumerians built impressive temples to these gods and had many personal and physical encounters with them just like many of the biblical characters had with the God of the Old Testament. It is important to note that these were the first gods in recorded human history that expressed their obsession with gold and made it clear that all the gold of the planet belonged to them. It was this same message that was passed on to the Spanish conquistadores when they began to terrorise the native American people. The Spaniards came across unthinkable amounts of stored gold, gold artefacts and entire golden cities. They were told unequivocally by the native Americans that "all the gold belongs to the gods".

The one thing the Sumerians did really well was to capture their activities on clay tablets. The first calendar, poetry, recipes, court proceedings, music, and especially their history and tales of their origins, which included the creation of Earth and the solar system in a group of tablets called the *Enuma Elish* or 'Epic of Creation'. The Sumerians explain in great detail how man was created, how the gods made him in their image, with the single purpose to toil in the gold mines of the ABZU, or southern Africa, for thousands of years. It also explains how Lord ENKI, who was in charge of the gold mining, chose his domain and built a strong fortress in the ABZU,

Top left: MS 3026 Sumerian Flood Story. The story of the great flood as told by the Sumerians. This tablet introduces Ziusudra, the Sumerian Noah, and the events that led to the world being destroyed in a great flood of water.

Top right: The Sumerian King List – tablet. One of the most famous Sumerian tablets. It lists 149 kings and rulers on planet Earth. Ten rulers before the flood - spanned some 240,000 years. It outlines when Kingdom was lowered to Earth from Heaven by the Anunnaki or biblical Nephilim. The list also outlines the coming to Earth of the biblical Anakim. It describes how Ninurta, youngest son of Enlil, the biblical YAHWEH destroyed Sodom & Gomorrah. This event was captured in great detail in another collection of tablets called the Erra Epos.

which would be somewhere in Zimbabwe.

This description matches the profile of the Great Zimbabwe Ruins perfectly and is one of the many Sumerian translations referring to mining activity in ancient times and the fate of modern humans.

"… Great rivers there rapidly flowed. An abode by the flowing waters Enki for himself established." He established a fortress for his house and other places where the workers would live and "where the bowels of the Earth to enter… Place of deepness he determined, for the heroes into Earth's bowels to descend" to extract the gold. (Sitchin – Lost Book of Enki)

Could these ancient stone ruins be the settlements of the early humans enslaved to work in ancient gold mines? Could the ancient **Adam's Calendar** at Kaapschehoop in Mpumalanga, South Africa be the centrepiece of this era? Could some of the more elaborate and impressive ruins, like Great Zimbabwe, be the fortress remains of the ancient gods who controlled the gold mining operations? These notions are not as crazy as they may seem at first glance.

We need to establish the levels of credibility of the Sumerian tablets, and how far we are prepared to believe them. Thousands of scholars have gone to great lengths to show how accurate the Sumerian knowledge was. There is no suspicion among scholars that the information captured by the Sumerians was intended to deceive us, since we still apply much of their knowledge in our daily lives today. But what has become highly questionable, is the selective approach by many scholars towards the content of the tablets.

On the one hand we are taught how impressive the Sumerian civilisation was and how accurate their science was. But in the same breath our historians tend to disregard all that was written by the same meticulous Sumerians about our human origins, God, Eden, Adam and Eve, and much of what we read in the Bible many thousands of years later. I struggle to understand why some scholars choose to disregard the information shared by the Sumerians about the early humans; the conditions they lived in and their quest for gold in distant parts of the world. Once again, it seems to be, simply because it does not fit their rosy model of human history.

Most of our western history is based on Judeo-Christian religion and the early historians mostly fell into this category. While many of them have been exposed as being fraudulent, we still accept their viewpoints in our history books today and base our knowledge on those early fraudulent accounts. Some wrote with absolute certainty about events in the past, documenting fine details of who did what… and who said what… some 1,000 years after the event, as if they were there to witness it. And these are the historic manuscripts upon which we base much of our perception of what happened in the past.

Here is a simple example of how one of the most famous historic figures was hijacked by historians of the past and remains entrapped in that character until today. Remember that the biblical Gods (Elohim) interacted and communicated with the early people they had chosen. According to the Bible, Abraham was one such person. He travelled long and far guided by his God, crossing the whole of the Near East. He built a powerful army because God gave him advanced weapons with which he could slay other armies many times the size of his. He also acquired immense wealth and controlled vast amounts of land given to him by God. Other rulers and kings feared him because his God was more powerful than theirs. Quite frankly, the whole story of Abraham is highly suspicious, his activities defy any logic and the destruction of Sodom and Gomorrah is a turning point in our Judeo-Christian past when compared to the Sumerian account of that important event.

After all, the Sumerians got their instructions and

Above: A side view of the two main calendar stones of Adam's Calendar. Maybe we should start calling it Enki's Calendar, since numerous psychics have independently confirmed our research that the Sumerian deity Enki was responsible for its construction. Notice the unusually thick lichen growth on the taller of the two monoliths. An indication of its true age.

information from their gods, just like Abraham and Moses received information from their god. We should also remember that Abraham was not a Jew, but a Sumerian from a town called Ur and he features prominently in Sumerian history. So who was Abraham's god, and who were the Sumerian gods? They were the same group of deities described in detail in the Sumerian tablets and echoed in the Bible some 2,500 years later.

As far back as 1925 **Nature** magazine broke the story of irrefutable links between Sumerian and Indus Valley civilisations.

"The Indo-Sumerian Seals Deciphered: discovering Sumerians of Indus Valley as Phoenicians, Barats, Goths and Famous Vedic Aryans, 3100 – 2300 BC. COL. WADDELL, the well-known authority on Tibet, has stepped in where archaeologists, as yet, fear to tread. He has produced an interpretation of the remarkable seals which were found, with other relics suggesting an affinity with ancient Sumeria, at Mohenjo Daro and Harappa in the Indus Valley, and illustrated and described by Sir John Marshall, Director of the Archaeological Survey of India." *(Nature – 5 Sept 1925)*

This is a crucial bit of information because various scholars like Cyril Hromnik, Brenda Sullivan and Sangomas like Credo Mutwa have written in detail about the symbols that link Sumerians, Indus Valley, Egypt and South Africa. The only mystery we need to resolve is the fact that the artefacts and petroglyphs in South Africa are many thousands of years older than any of the northern hemisphere civilisations.

The African - Sumerian Connection

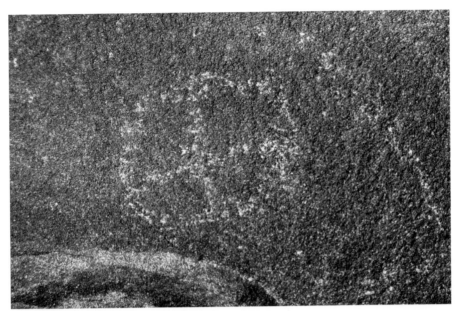

Above: A petroglyph of a winged disk in South Africa. This carving pre-dates all those of northern civilisations and suggests that the origin of this symbol is also in southern Africa.

Above: The original Sumerian winged disk was a simple cross in a circle with lines that represented wings attached to the sides. This evolved in various forms in the Near East and Egypt.

Above: Another adaptation of the winged disk showing a more advanced cross in the centre. This image is seen in many Sumerian seals, often hovering above the subject.

Is it possible that the early Africans worshipped the same Sumerian gods many thousands of years before the Sumerians themselves? According to Credo Mutwa, that is exactly what happened. During September 2008 I visited Credo and his wife Virginia at their home. We spent most of the day exploring many issues which included the murky origins of humankind; the lost civilisations of southern Africa; the importance of the sacred site we call *Adam's Calendar*; and many more fascinating topics which most people would probably frown at. During our chat Credo highlighted various important events to me.

The most significant was that southern Africa is indeed the cradle of humankind. By this I do not mean the cradle of 'hominid kind' as many scholars often suggest, but most certainly the cradle of modern humans – Homo sapiens – thinking man – the Sumerian *Adamu* or the biblical *Adam*. He also pointed out that this is the home of the original *Abantu* people, long before anyone had ever imagined. When Credo talks about the ancient Zulu, or African tradition/culture, he is actually referring to the FIRST people; the progenitors of all humans; the original Bantu – long before the establishment of the many Bantu tribes as we know them today.

While modern historians tell us that the Bantu migrated to the south from north-west Africa, starting some 2,000 years ago, our evidence shows that the ancestors and progenitors of the Bantu; the original humans, lived here long before that time. During various global disasters that spanned more than 60,000 years, those early humans migrated north, which is often called the "exodus from Africa". The most likely cause for this important event was the 'super-volcano' which erupted at Lake Toba in Sumatra. This giant explosion was only recently detected by scientists and they estimate that the prevailing winds carried most of the dust and poisonous gasses westwards, towards eastern and southern Africa. All you need to do is look on a global map or Google Earth and you will quickly realise that there is very little in the path of the billions of tonnes of dust, except the flat Indian ocean.

Scientists estimate that this eruption took place between 65,000 and 75,000 years ago. It was so massive that it would have caused a mini ice-age. The most affected areas would have been southern Africa, where the first civilisation lived and functioned very successfully. This was most likely the trigger that caused the exodus of the FIRST people from southern Africa into the rest of the world. They took with them all their traditions and customs, which included the sacred symbols and imagery. For over 200,000 years these FIRST people carved these images into stones and rock faces of the mountains of southern Africa. These included the many symbols that later emerged in the Egyptian and Sumerian civilisations, like the *winged planet/disk* and the *ankh*. They took with them the knowledge of building with stone, which was refined over millennia in other parts of the world. We should therefore not be surprised when we find stone circle ruins all over the planet, since this was

the most basic structure known to the FIRST people before they dispersed throughout the world.

Several thousand years later they started to migrate south to their original birthplace, not even realising that this is where they had initially come from.

Linda Tucker covers many more interesting aspects revealed to her by Credo Mutwa in her brilliant book *'Children of the Sun God'* which includes the FIRST people and their place in human history, right here at the southern tip of Africa.

But who were the first and original *Abantu* people? Where did they get their name from? Scholars have been arguing about the origins of the word *Bantu* or *Abantu* for decades. Some scholars like Cyril Hromnik suggest its origins lie in the Sanskrit word *'bandhu'*, meaning brother, relative, kinsman. The bottom line is that there are no obvious answers but only speculation by various scholars, most of whom have not taken all the evidence into account. How could they? Until now it was thought that southern Africa was a barren land filled with a handful of hunter-gatherers who somehow survived for thousands of years. No-one could have guessed that there are many lost cities covered

Above: Some examples of the Indus Valley script – as yet undeciphered. Close similarities can be found between the many petroglyphs in South Africa. But the South Africa petroglyphs are much older.

Above: The Anglo-Saxon runes also show great similarities to the petroglyphs in South Africa and the Indus script.

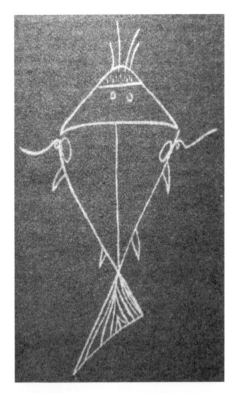

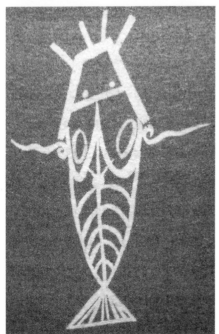

Above: Images show a Dogon drawing of a fish coming out of the water. It did not represent the simple act of fishing but something much more aligned with creation.

by the sands of time, consisting of millions of ancient circular stone structures, all linked together by a mysterious grid of stone walls.

The root of the word 'abantu' is 'ntu'. This little root has caused many heated debates in academic circles over the decades. The two places on Earth where this 'ntu' root is most obviously found, is in southern/east Africa and the ancient Sumerian civilisation. Biblical historian and professor of theology, Zecharia Sitchin has devoted a lifetime of research to the Sumerians and the obscure origins of humankind. Sitchin's many books outline the pantheon of Sumerian gods, their relationships with each other and their control of planet Earth in great detail. I was therefore not surprised when Credo Mutwa launched into his own explanation regarding the source of the name *Aba'ntu*.

All the Sumerian gods had spouses or wives, whose names often resembled those of the

Right: A seal with Indus Valley script, as yet un-deciphered, with a very similar fish. There are many similarities between petroglyphs in South Africa and images used by both Dogon and Indus people. But the South African petroglyphs are much older, probably way over 100,000 years old if judged by the erosion around the cracks through the glyphs.

male gods. ENLIL'S spouse was NINLIL; ENKI'S wife was NINKI; and the wife of the supreme Sumerian god ANU, was A'NTU. So now we come to realise that not only do the ancient symbols originate in southern Africa, but the first link to the ancient gods, who came to rule over the whole of the Near East many thousands of years later, comes from the link to the Sumerian goddess A'NTU. Herein lies the link that ties all the ancient civilisations to each other, starting with the FIRST people, in southern Africa who worshipped a Sumerian goddess called A'NTU. It is astonishing to discover that ancient Zulu culture and religion, including those of all other Bantu tribes, is directly linked to the Sumerians. Credo concludes that *Abantu* is derived from the Sumerian goddess A'NTU and simply means ABA'NTU – the children/people of A'NTU. A Sumerian goddess who loved the ABZU – southern Africa, where the gold came from.

Petroglyphs

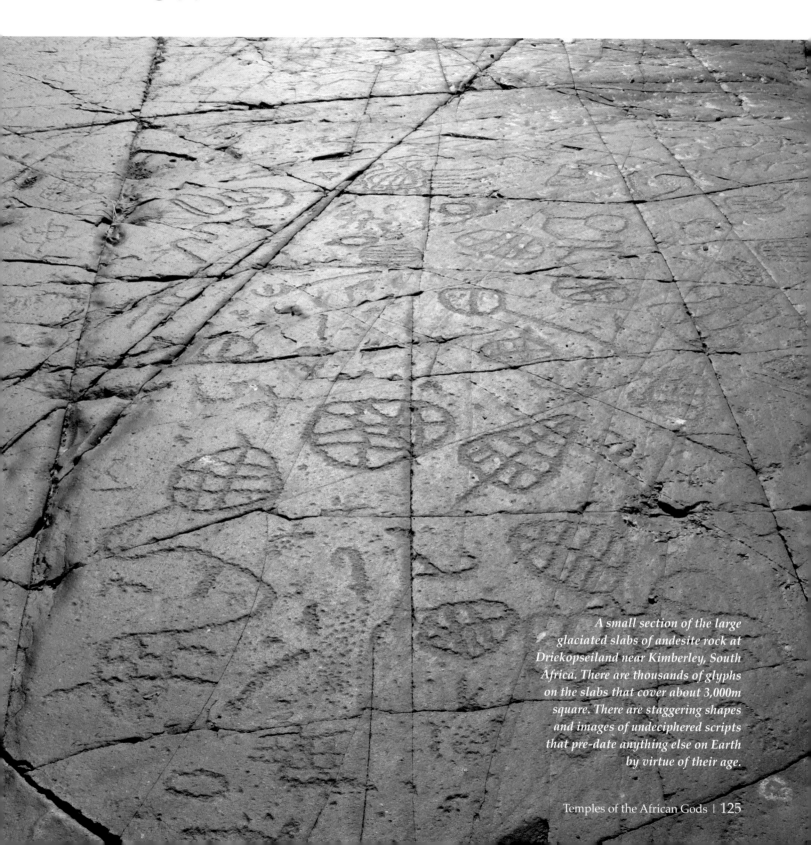

A small section of the large glaciated slabs of andesite rock at Driekopseiland near Kimberley, South Africa. There are thousands of glyphs on the slabs that cover about 3,000m square. There are staggering shapes and images of undeciphered scripts that pre-date anything else on Earth by virtue of their age.

Above: Cross in a circle plus an oval shape dissected in half, near Carolina, SA.

Top right: Cross in a circle and the oval dissected at Driekopseiland. Showing that the same symbols were used across vast distances by ancient people in South Africa. The dissected oval is a representation of the moon goddess, while the cross in a circle represents the Lord of Light. (Sullivan & Mutwa)

Above: Sumerian seal showing a script similar to carvings at Driekopseiland, South Africa.

Above: Indus script seal also showing a distinct star in a circle. The Sumerians also used an 8-pointed star in a circle as representation of the planet of the gods.

Left: Five distinctly different shapes indicating a conscious written script much earlier that any other script ever found. It shows great similarity to later Sumerian and Indus script and could even be the prototype for Chinese style of writing. (Driekopseiland).

Above: The five-pointed star, as in the extreme left symbol, is also an Egyptian symbol of kingship associated with a link to the divine – specifically the god Baal.

Top right: A cross, or possibly even an ankh, inside a hexagon, with concentric circles outward. This can be interpreted as quite a complex image, involving the knowledge of matter while the hexagon represents a star tetrahedron. The ankh is synonymous with sound frequency, in the generation of energy, inside concentric circles as amplification chambers. Basic knowledge of energy that we do not posses today. Once again the erosion indicates its extreme age of over 100,000 years at least.

Right: A very complex carving by a well informed person, a long, long time ago. A serpent, representing vibrational frequency or ohm shape (Ω) – also approximating the OM shape, inside a pentagon, with a star above it. The horseshoe shape is often depicted as one of the six syllables of OM. The OM is regarded as the prime sound of creation, because of its vibrational frequency. The serpent has always been seen as the creator in most ancient cultures. The shape of the pentagon is associated with the creator and the divine because of the Phi factor, or 1.618… ratio. The dot above the serpent could represent a star like Sirius or another star associated with creation and worship among ancient African cultures. Similar horseshoe shapes are found among the ruins.

Right: An ancient coin from Greece showing an identical serpent in the same horseshoe shape. The recurrence of this serpent shape and shapes among the ruins were not accidental, but shows an understanding of sound and vibrational frequency.

Above: Carvings in a cave in Limpopo province, northern South Africa. The cross is identical to Sumerian crosses found in numerous Sumerian seals.

Above: Petroglyphs found near Lydenburg, South Africa. Perfectly drilled holes in very specific sequence, probably marking the movements of some stars or planets, or maybe the moon. Probably a calendar of some kind. How they drilled the holes remains a mystery.

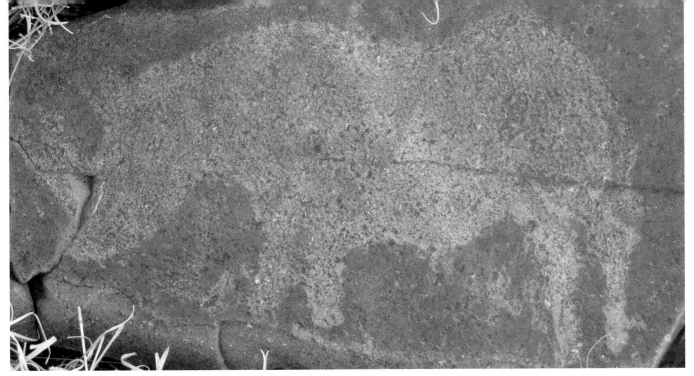

Above: A rhino carving at Wildebeeskuil, South Africa. The cracks through the carving once again indicate that it is much older than the 2000 years ascribed to it.

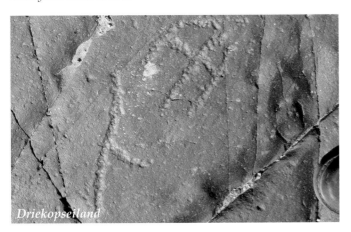

Driekopseiland

Mpuluzi, close to the Swaziland border.

Wolmeransstad

Lambda symbols scattered on rocks around South Africa are identical to those found in Anglo-Saxon runes and Indus script. The symbol is not yet understood but its appearance at locations separated by vast distances indicates that the symbol carried an important meaning.

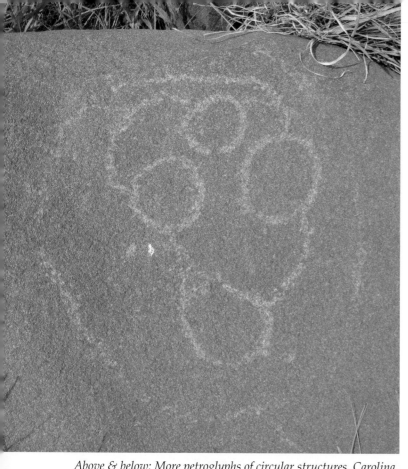

Above & below: More petroglyphs of circular structures, Carolina.

Above & bottom right: Carving of a stone circle complex, near Waterval Boven. It is very similar to the archaeological sketches from Nooitgedacht Dam, resembling a cluster of grapes. Note, the absence of entrances. Many circles all joined together by channels or roads. Now that we understand the energy generating principle, it seems that this is a good example of an early diagram of an energy generating complex. The energy is channelled via the channels that connect them all together, to create a continuous energy grid. The simple non-polar, or radiant energy would have been used for everything as we imagine it today – and more. It is not a dangerous form of energy like the polar electricity we use today.

Top left: Wave forms like these are associated with water and life. But it could also represent the knowledge of frequency and its application as the primary source of energy – whether it was from the sun or emanating from Mother Earth.

Centre left: Two examples of the same image from different locations. They are very similar to the Dogon people's images of the germination of matter, or creation, indicated by the incomplete circle and the rays of energy emanating from it.

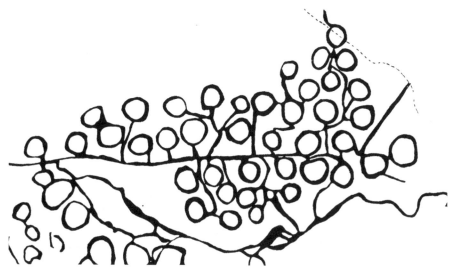

Aerial Views

One of the largest ruins we have been researching. It measures 150m across. No entrances have been found into the original structure. The only entrance found seems to be created by later inhabitants.

The extended web that once connected all these ruins
is now not visible and well covered by soil and grass.
Note the horseshoe, ohm-like shape that faces the
spiral of the large ruin – suggesting once again the
manipulation of sound and energy.

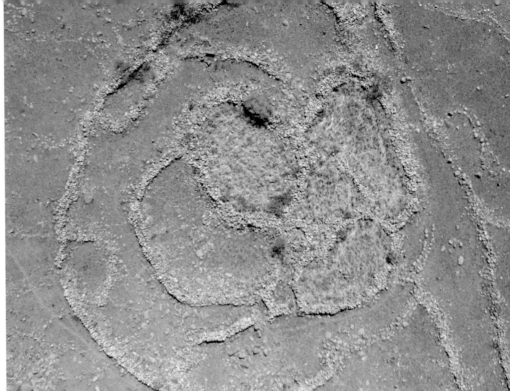

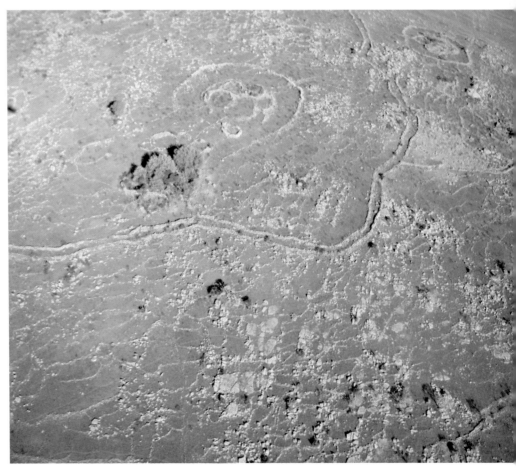

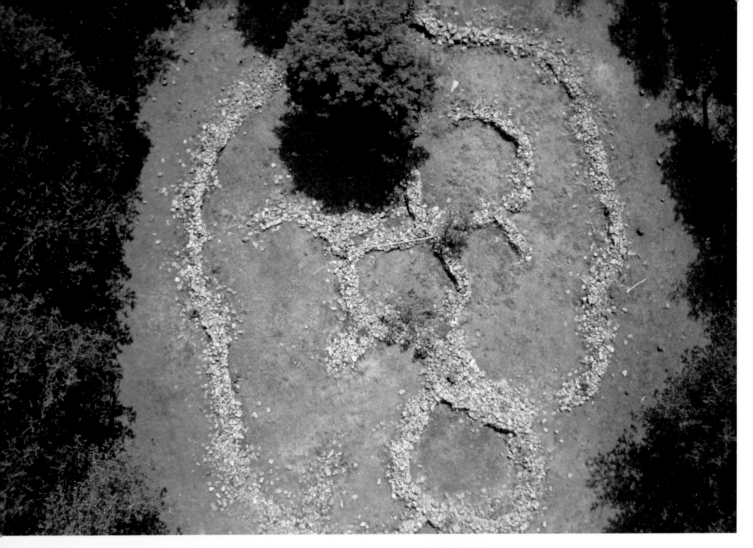

Thousands of ruins are in forestry areas,
well out of sight. Many thousands
have been destroyed and continue to be
destroyed. Although SAPPI has become
aware of this and is involved with the
MaKomati Foundation to protect and clear
some of the more accessible and prominent
ruins.

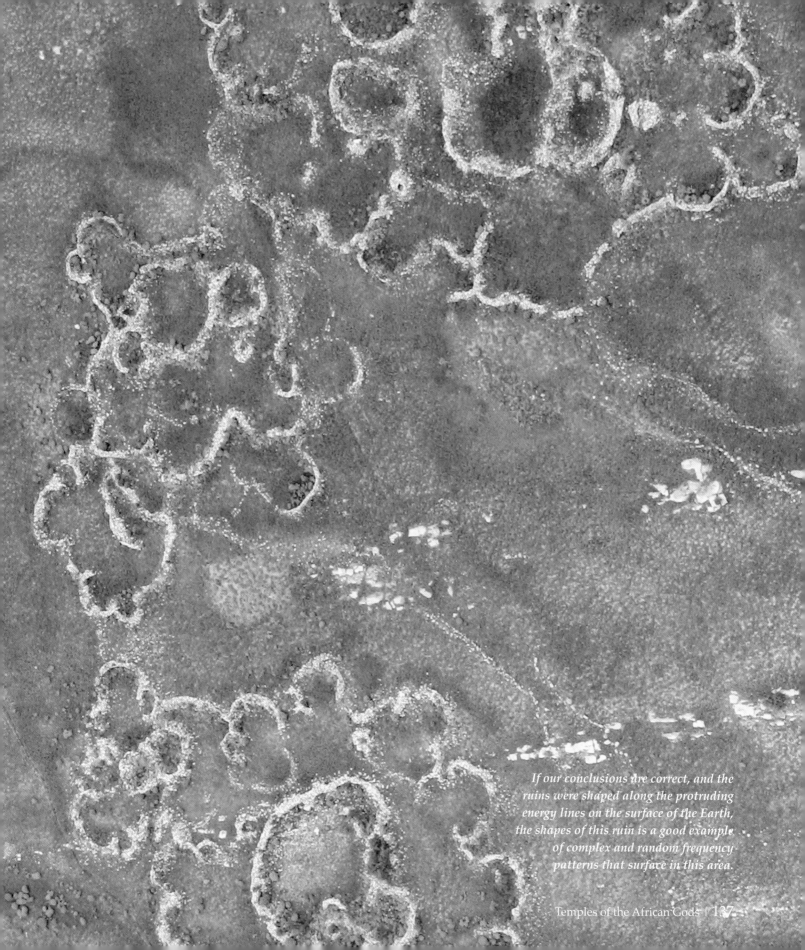

If our conclusions are correct, and the ruins were shaped along the protruding energy lines on the surface of the Earth, the shapes of this ruin is a good example of complex and random frequency patterns that surface in this area.

Notice the concentric circles probably acting as resonant amplification, and the extended web of walls that surrounds the central circle.

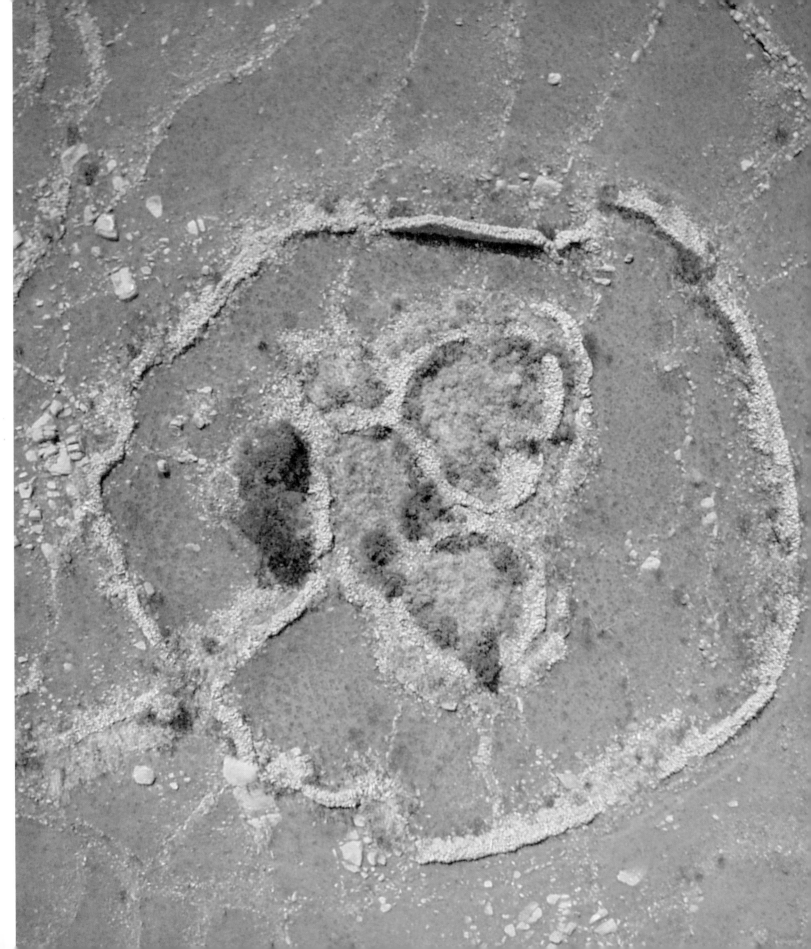

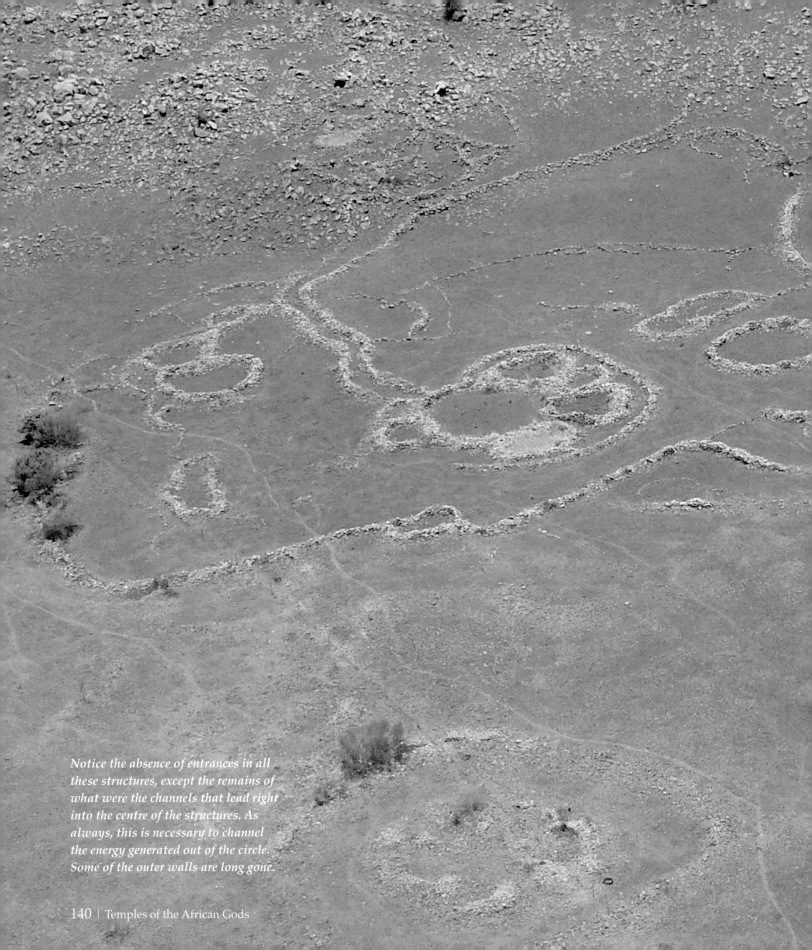

Notice the absence of entrances in all these structures, except the remains of what were the channels that lead right into the centre of the structures. As always, this is necessary to channel the energy generated out of the circle. Some of the outer walls are long gone.

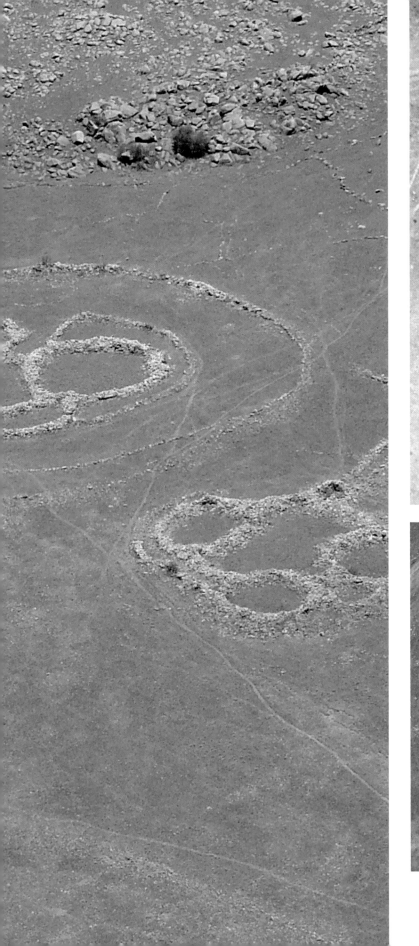

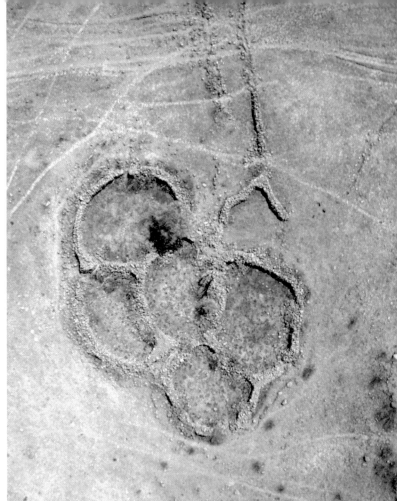

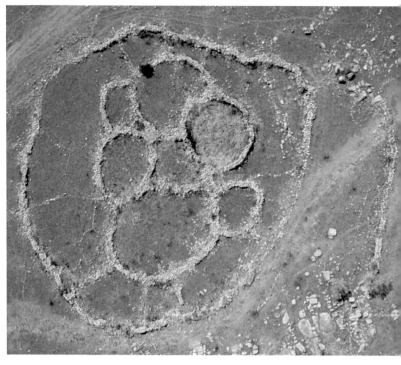

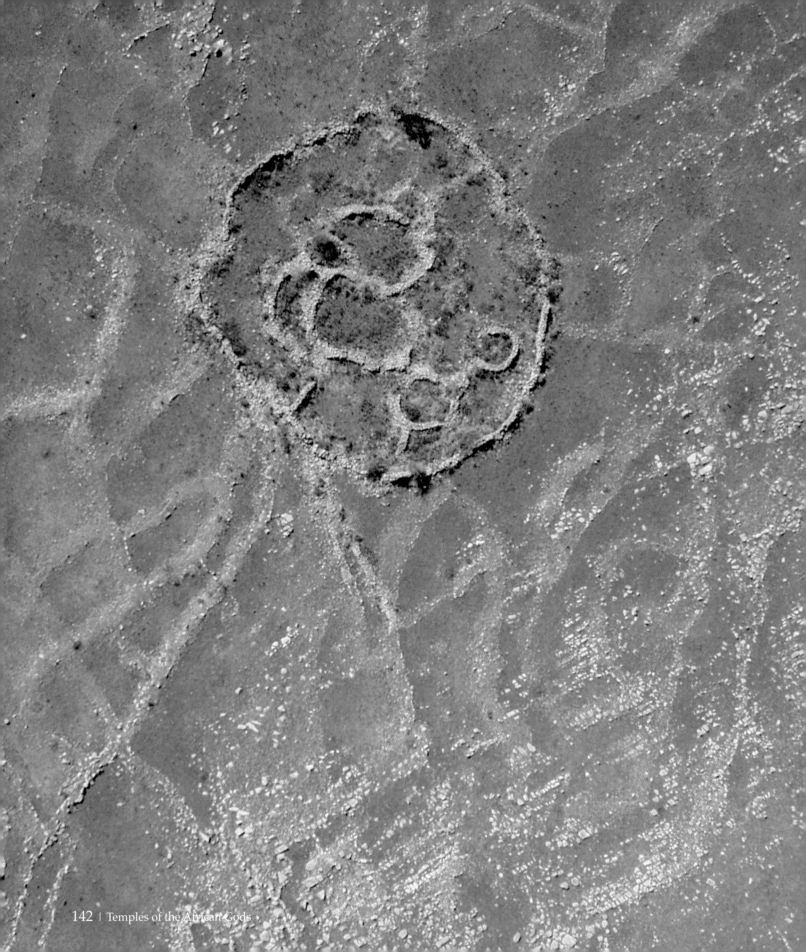

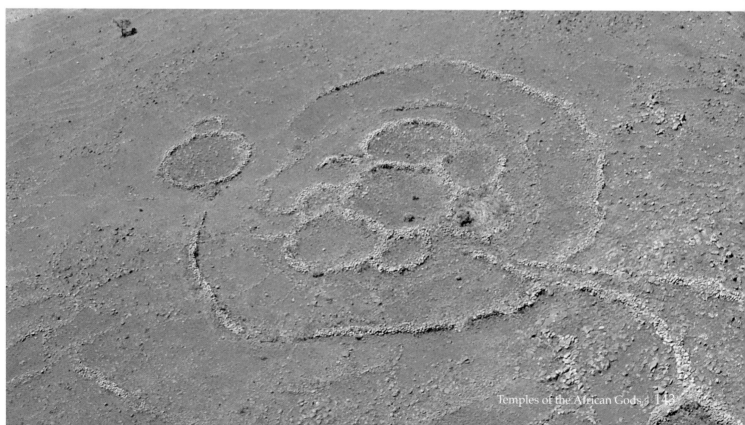

Temples of the African Gods | 143

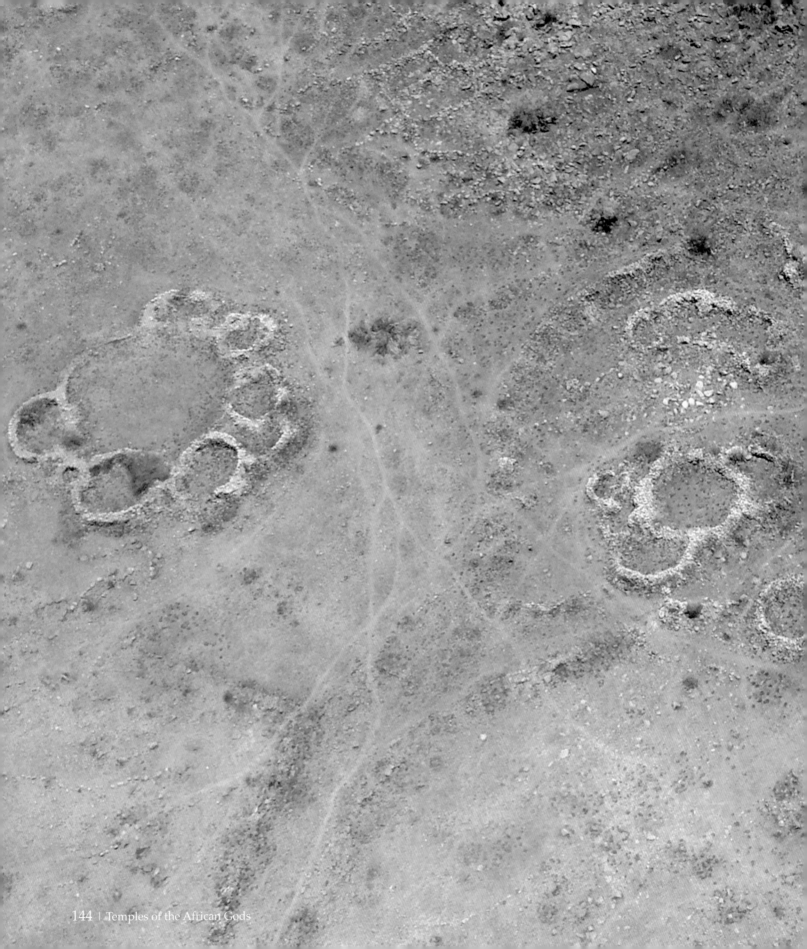

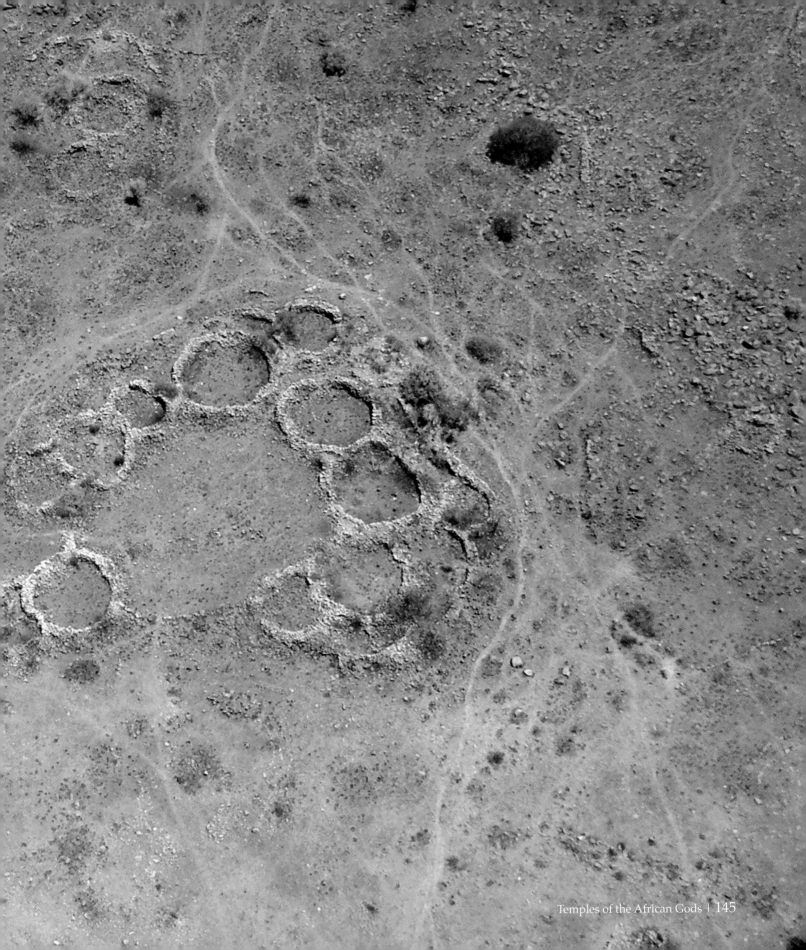

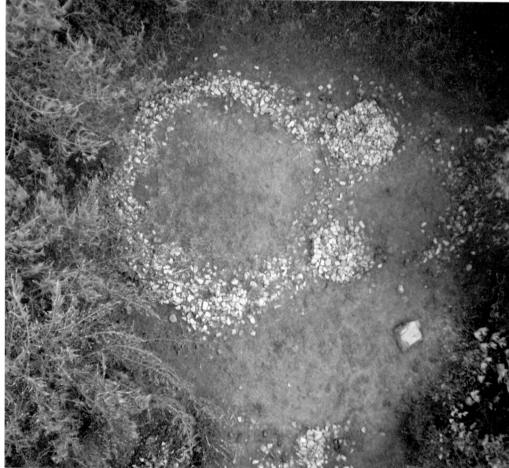

Top right: A recognised symbol of fertility in Hindu tradition.

Bottom: Another distinct example of the OM shape, symbolising the influence of Indian miners, or the ruin of the FIRST people who understood the usage of sound very well, and who passed this knowledge on to all other civilisations, including the Hindus.

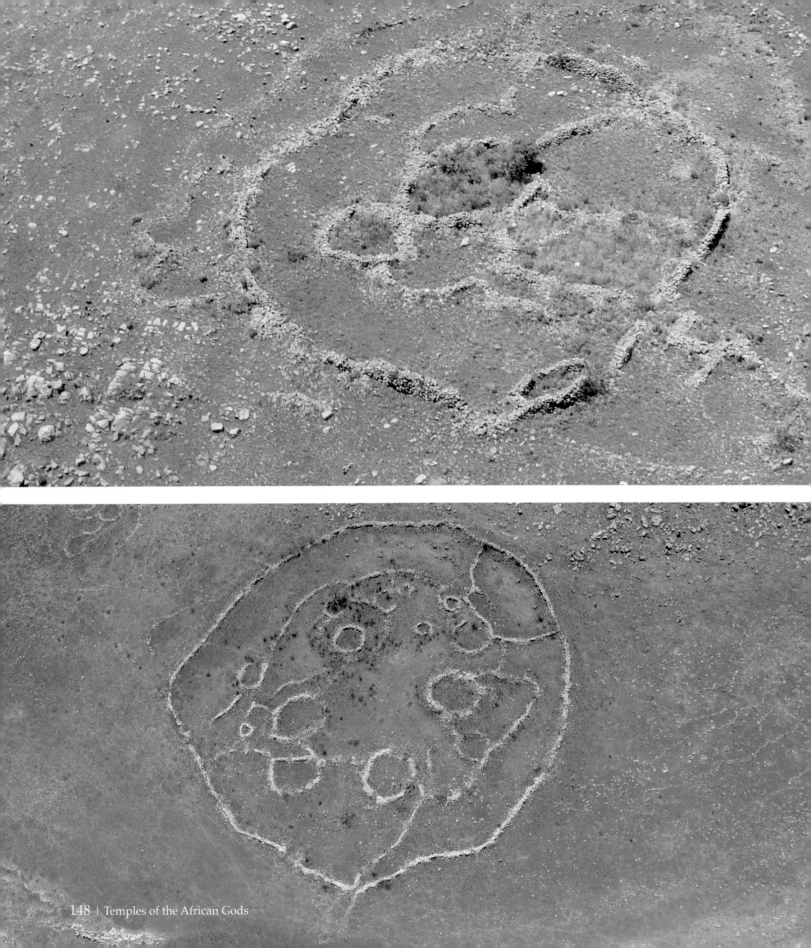

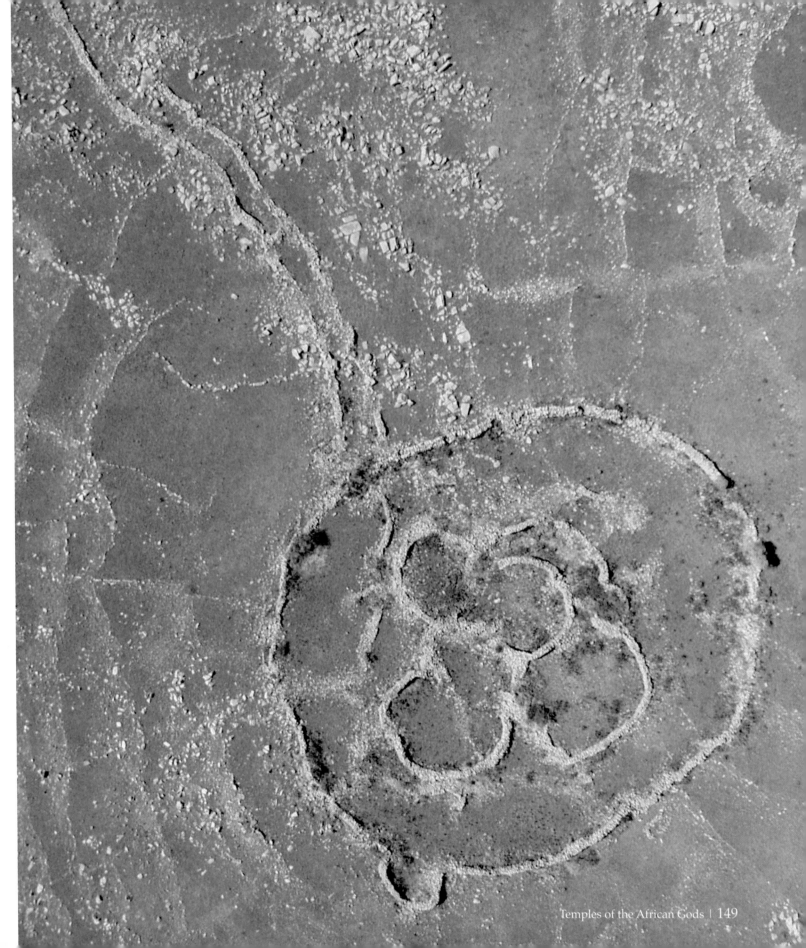

Temples of the African Gods | 149

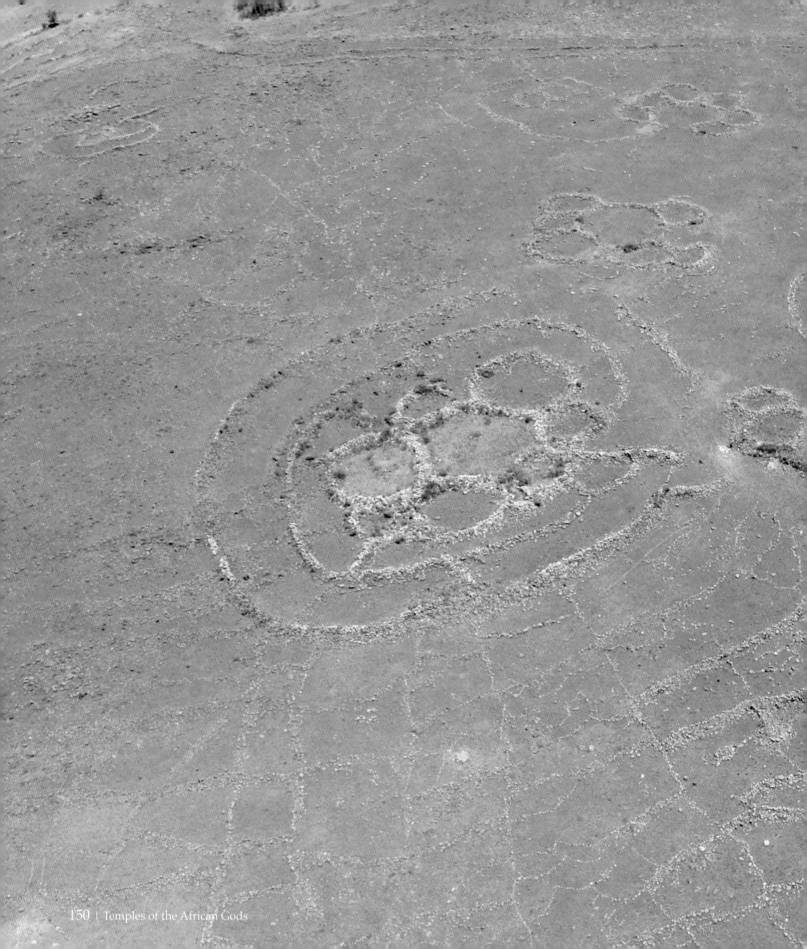

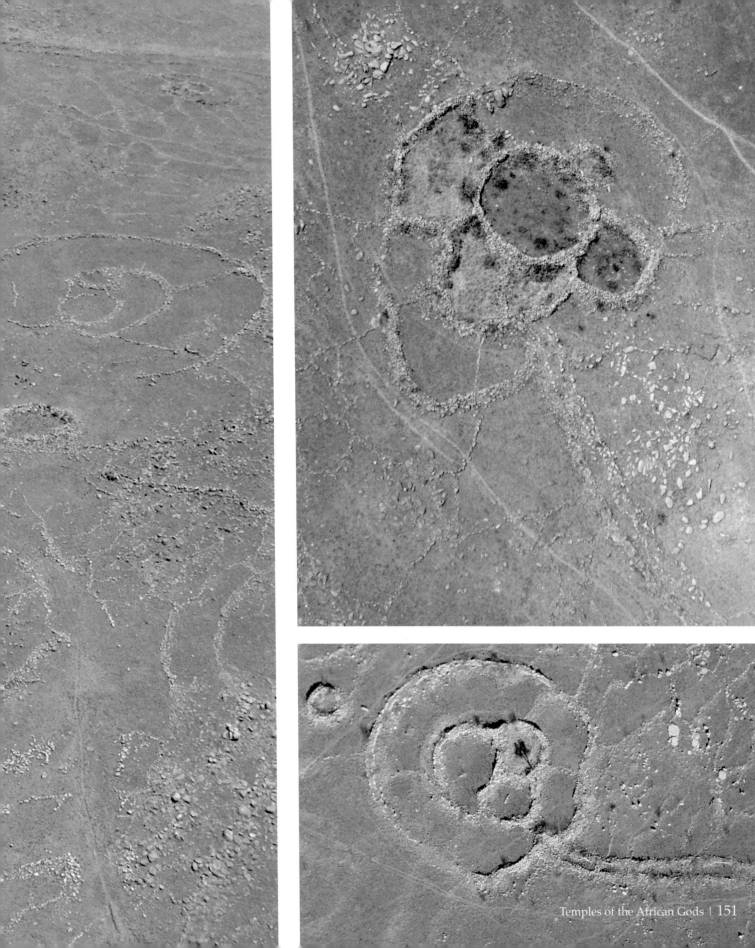

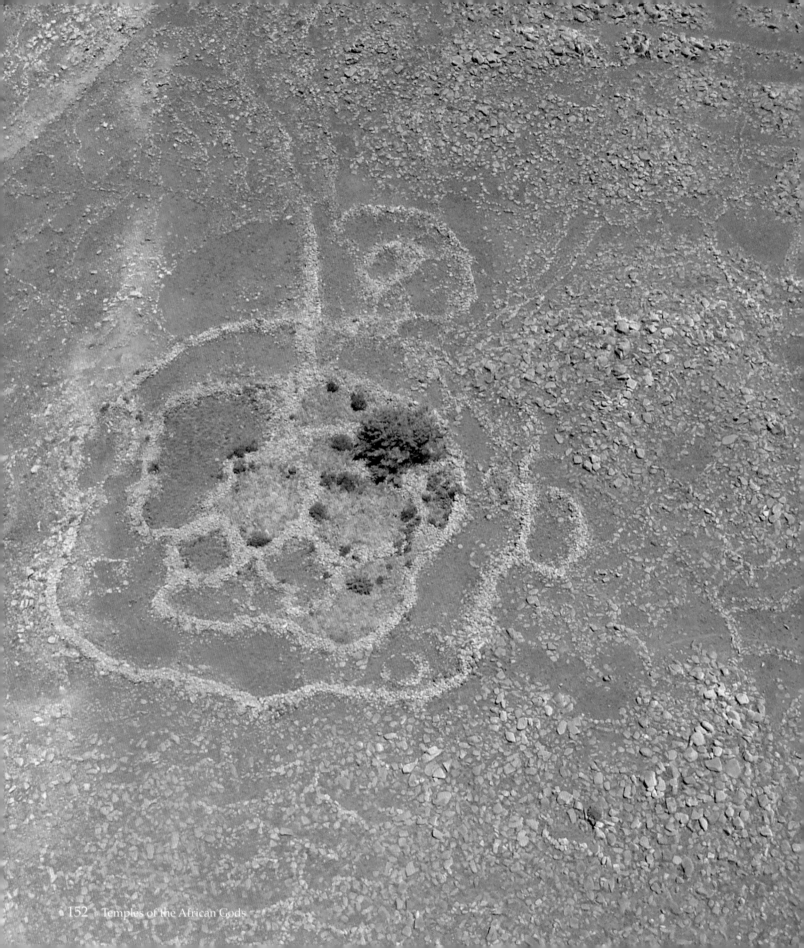

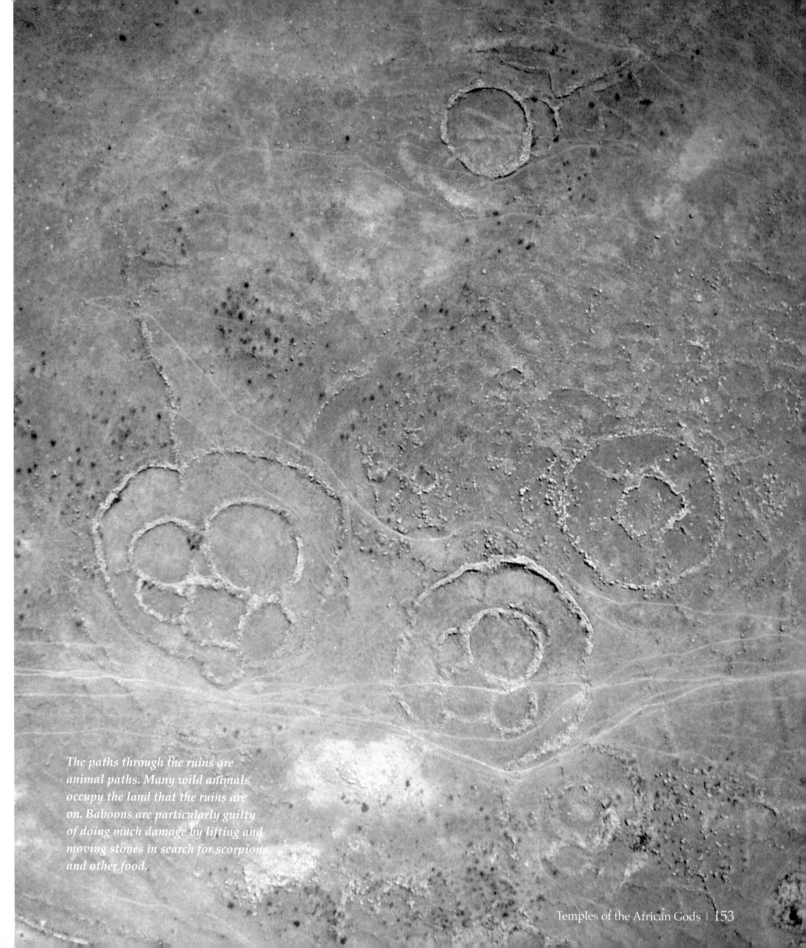

The paths through the ruins are animal paths. Many wild animals occupy the land that the ruins are on. Baboons are particularly guilty of doing much damage by lifting and moving stones in search for scorpions and other food.

The greater web of stone and the channels that once linked these structures on top of the mountain is hardy visible. Fish fossils have been found in large numbers on the mountain tops in this area, indicating support for the Great Flood that devastated the civilisation between 10,000 and 14,000 years ago.

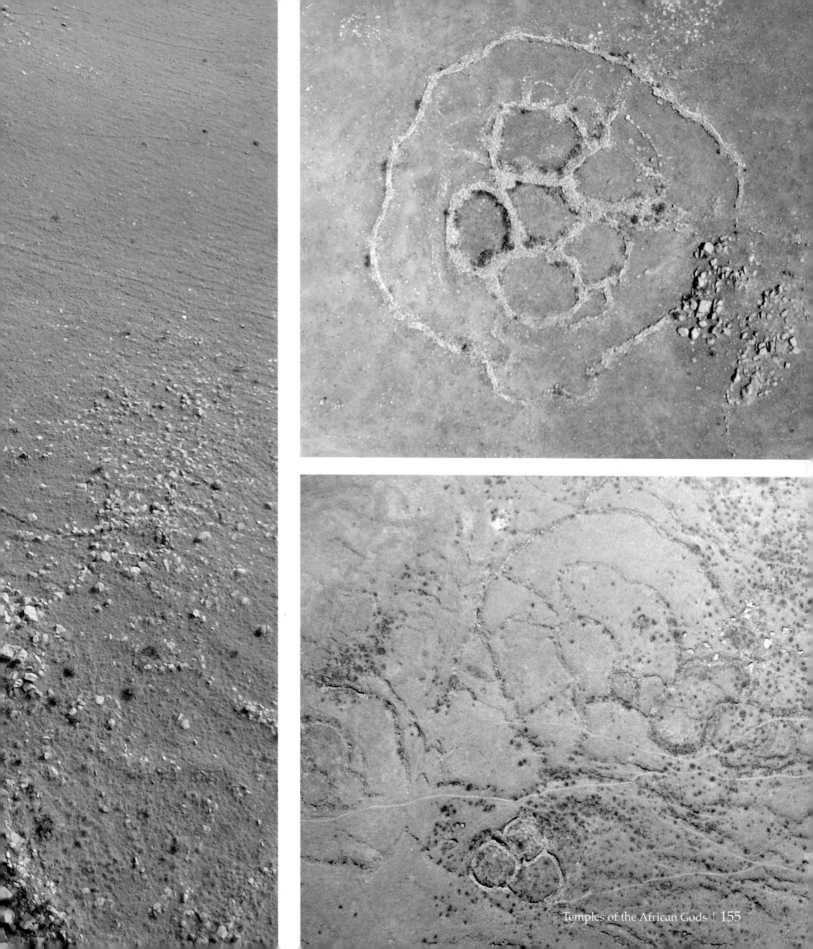

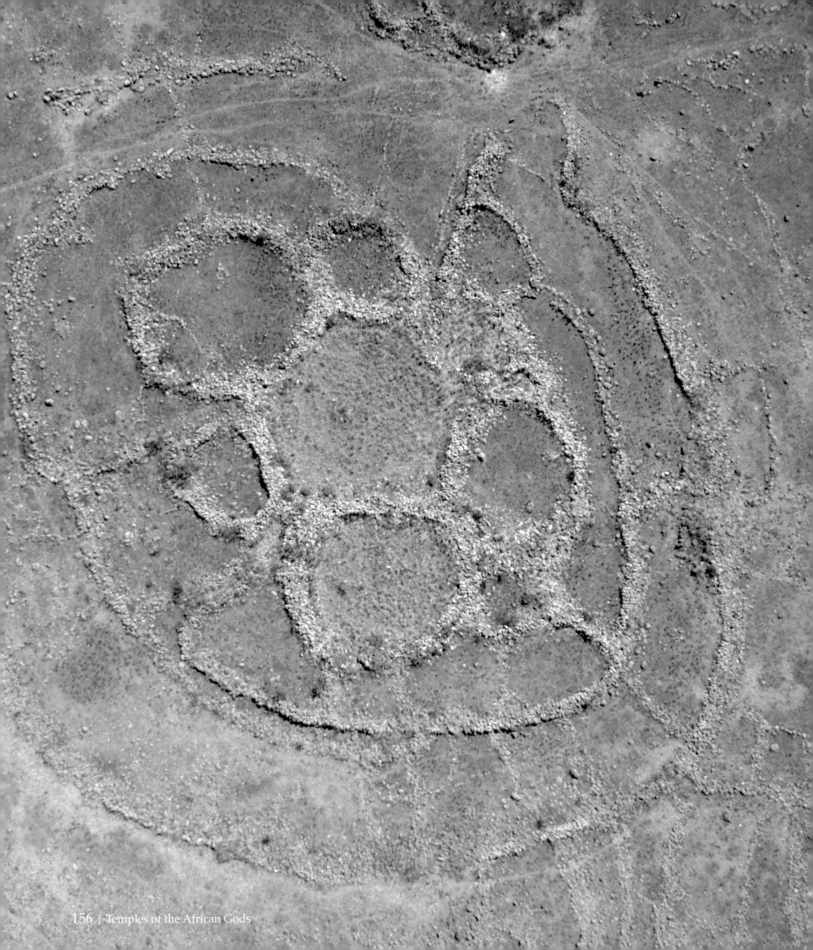

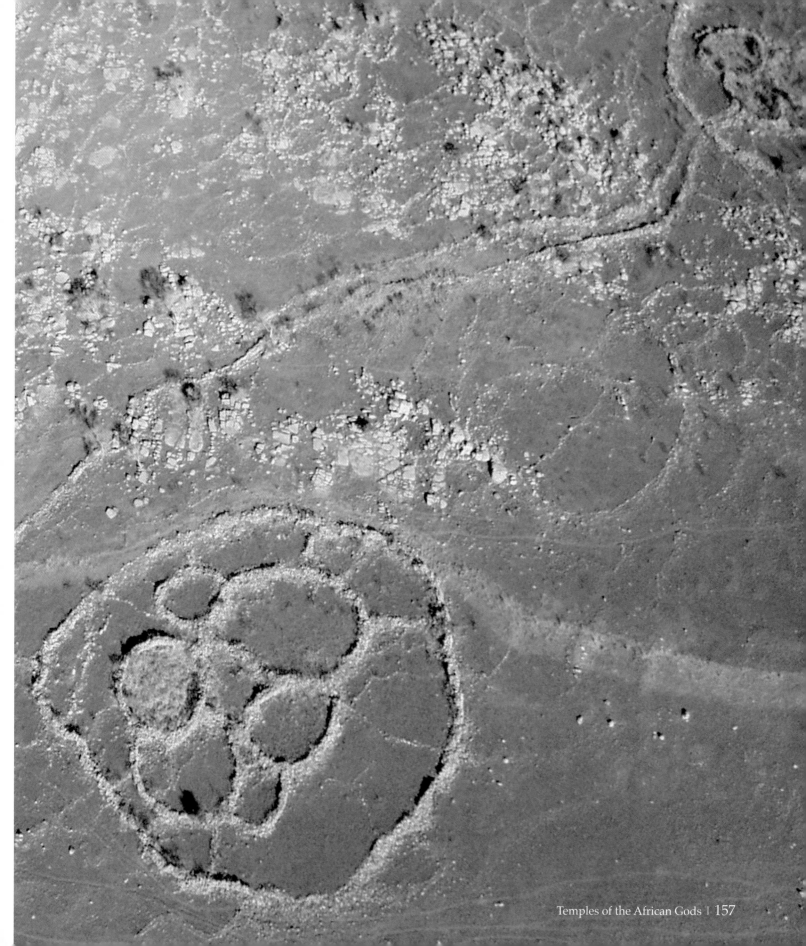

A spectacular example of terraces, channels and stone circles, covering several mountains near Waterval Boven.

Monoliths

Opposite: The lost civilisation was obsessed with monoliths. This is a breathtaking example of a bird-shape monolith near Belfast, South Africa. There are obvious links to the well-known and mysterious Zimbabwe birds. Notice the wing that was once carved onto the lower body of the bird, greatly resembling the wings on the Zimbabwe birds, placed low on the body.

Top: A strange accumulation of rectangular rocks carved and placed in some kind of arrangement. Meaning not established.

Bottom: Nick van Noordwyk, who is 6ft 6in tall, stands at the mysterious bird monolith indicating its size.

All pictures: The recurring shapes of carved stones at many of the ruins. A broader base with a long narrow neck and head. We believe that these are the early and basic prototypes of what became the more refined Zimbabwe birds.

This is one of our greatest discoveries yet, which allows us to speculate about the very old age of the ruins. The patina on this broken monolith has re-grown to about 2mm thickness. It is our estimate that this kind of patina growth will not happen in less than 100,000 years. Although no scientific study exists to verify this, we are about to conduct an experiment on the growth of this particular patina with the Nelson Mandela Metropolitan University in Port Elizabeth.

Polished monoliths and stones such as this one are linked directly to the Hindu worship of Lord Shiva. We believe it has its origins in southern Africa and could be linked to the polishing of gold for the gods by the FIRST people of the vanished civilisation.

A giant fallen monolith – more than 3.5m tall.

Top: *A 5-metre tall monolith near Dullstroom, South Africa. Once again it resembles the basic bird shape of the prototype bird statues and monoliths. A broad base that narrows to the top.*

Bottom: *Johan admires one of many built-in stones into the walls of certain ruins.*

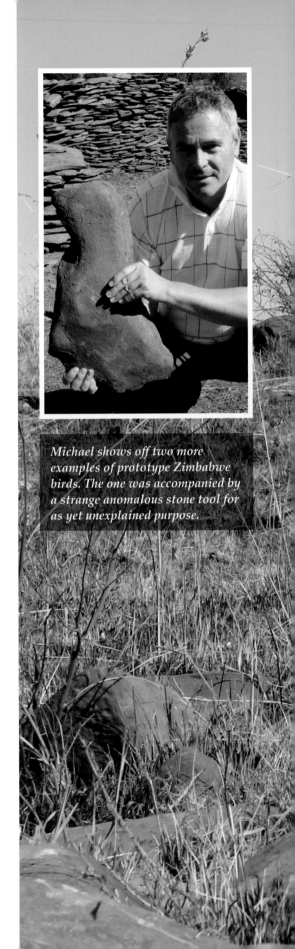

Michael shows off two more examples of prototype Zimbabwe birds. The one was accompanied by a strange anomalous stone tool for as yet unexplained purpose.

Above: Another example of a built-in triangular stone into the wall of a large ruin. Triangular stones like this are associated with Hindu tradition and worship. But it seems that the Hindus also inherited their symbols from the FIRST people and the vanished civilisation of southern Africa. We can say this with some certainty because of the ages of the ruins and the tools found in these ruins. It is however possible that the Hindu gold miners adapted some of the ruins to their own needs. This is evident from new entrances created in many of the original structures.

Another wonderful example of a bird statue.

Some geologists are so baffled by the strange shapes of many of the tools and monoliths we have discovered, that they believe the ancient civilisation must have had some kind of ability to mould them like clay, by effecting their structural frequency, without actually carving them. If they understood the flow of energy as indicated by the stone circles, this notion is not as far-fetched as some may think.

Tools & Anomalies

Top: Credo Mutwa calls them Sacred Stones but these stones have been called many things. Most commonly called digging stones, used as weights attached to sticks for the purpose of digging for roots and food by Bantu settlers or hunter gatherers. This is an ignorant and preposterous suggestion. The fact that hundreds of thousands of these stones lie scattered throughout southern Africa is a huge mystery. Until we consider the use of vibrational frequency as energy, the same way that John Keely demonstrated in 1888. The holes in the stones are of different sizes and shapes and would generate a specific frequency when sound passes through it. They could well have been tools of the FIRST people in the construction of stone dwellings and mining of metals. Each sacred stone has a specific function and was probably calibrated to the specific frequency of its operator. John Keely showed the same when he pointed out that only he could use the vibration anti-gravity device which was calibrated to him only. The device was a basic trumpet-like instrument, which is basically a tube with a hole in it – just like our Sacred Stones.

Top right: A small statuette carved out of stone, about 15cm tall, found among stone tools at Waterval Boven. According to our estimate, this is by far the oldest statue on Earth.

Right: Large ritual stone phallus, 45cm long, found next to a stone circle ruin on top of a mountain, among many other Stone Age tools.

Left: The giant footprint in rough granite near Mpuluzi, South Africa, is the best example of an ancient unexplained phenomenon. This is not a hoax. Most archaeologists and scholars simply shy away from this discovery, which is not the kind of response one would expect from a true scientist. We have to examine this phenomenon to help us understand the real history of this planet. When the Bible talks about the Anakim, or giants on Earth, maybe this is what it was referring to.

Conclusion

This book was written and compiled purely to present a few highlights and the mystery of our ancient history. The collection of spectacular photographs leaves no doubt that something strange was happening in southern Africa many thousands of years ago. Our current civilisation is only beginning to see the tip of the proverbial iceberg of our ancient past. We trust that this will stimulate you to ask more questions, explore more and embark on a journey of discovery more fascinating than you could have ever imagined.

A NOTE OF GRATITUDE

In any process of research and discovery there is a great deal of work accompanied with the ups and downs that swing between depression and ecstasy. A journey like ours is not an easy one and could not be accomplished without the continuous support from a multitude of individuals and organisations. Some people contributed to our discoveries in many ways, sometimes completely unaware of their actions. We compiled a list of those people who crossed our path in the process of making these startling discoveries. To all of you, and those who we may have omitted, we extend our most sincere gratitude. Please keep exploring and spread your own passion.

Paul van Niekerk and all the farmers whose land we use in our exploration, Brian Young, Bruce & Roelie Pretorius, Prof. Pieter Wagener, Mike van Niekerk, Theunis & Ben Niewoudt, Linda Pampallis, Angie Shackleford, Matt Louw, Thompsons Travel, Win Saunders, Nicola Wilson, Rudi & Petro du Plessis, Reinette van Niekerk, the people of Kaapschehoop, Andy Stadler, Johan Zietsman, Cyril Hromnik, SAPPI & Richard McArthy, Richard Green, Richard Wade, Willemien Hodgkinson, Fred Favar and the Working on Fire team, Gustav & Alex van Rensburg, DJ van Tonder, Willem de Swart, John Wallington, Frans Kruger, George van Gils, Merwyn Williams, Darryl Freeman, Peter and Rose Hobson, Nick van Noordwyk, Lily Hattingh, Peter Batistich, Bill Maliepaard; Junita Coetzee Ted Loukes, people of Waterval Boven and many more.

VISIT THE ANCIENT RUINS

A large display of unique artefacts and photographs can be viewed at the Stone Circle Bistro & Museum in Waterval Boven, Mpumalanga, South Africa.

We have initiated a variety of tours to the ruins.

To find out more email us on **info@makomati.com** or go to **www.makomati.com** or **www.adamscalendar.com**